THE
BIG
BOOK OF
BAKING

THE BIG BOOK OF BAKING

Your complete guide to
perfect baking every time

Love Food® is an imprint of Parragon Books Ltd

Parragon
Queen Street House
4 Queen Street
Bath BA1 1HE, UK

ISBN 978-1-4075-3966-9

Internal design by Simon Levy
Photography by Clive Streeter
Food styling by Angela Drake and Teresa Goldfinch
Introduction and additional recipes by Christine France

Printed in China

Notes for the reader

This book uses metric and imperial measurements. Follow the same units of measurement throughout; do not mix metric and imperial. All spoon measurements are level, unless otherwise stated; teaspoons are assumed to be 5 ml, and tablespoons are assumed to be 15 ml. Unless otherwise stated, milk is assumed to be full fat, eggs and individual fruits, such as bananas, are medium, and pepper is freshly ground black pepper.

Recipes using raw or lightly cooked eggs should be avoided by infants, the elderly, pregnant women, convalescents and anyone suffering from an illness. Pregnant and breast-feeding women are advised to avoid eating peanuts and peanut products.

CONTENTS

INTRODUCTION

Few types of cookery offer more rewards than home baking. Not only can you make irresistible sweet and savoury treats for your family and friends, but the actual hands-on process of baking is immensely satisfying, and you may be surprised at how much fun it can be. The basic skills are really easy to learn and you need very little in the way of special equipment to make some impressive cakes and bakes. All it needs is a little practice, and you'll get your baking confidence in no time!

While it's true that you can buy good-quality ready-made cakes these days, the satisfaction of baking your own, knowing exactly what ingredients they contain and even making them cheaper than you can buy them makes all the effort worthwhile. If you have children, baking is a great way to encourage them to start helping in the kitchen, and most children love to cook. Even toddlers can usually be given a simple job, as long as they're supervised by an adult. Try starting them off with an easy task like spooning mixture from a bowl into bun cases, for example, or arranging sweet decorations on top of a finished cake.

The Big Book of Baking contains all the recipes you need to enjoy baking, including some familiar classics and lots of new ideas too. You'll find recipes for a huge variety of cakes and bakes – including simple sponge cakes, special occasion cakes and gateaux, delicious desserts, irresistible biscuits, tempting traybakes and buns, sweet and savoury pies and tarts, classic breads and more unusual yeasted bakes with international flavours. All the recipes are thoroughly tested, with easy-to-follow instructions, so you can rely on them for good results every time. Every recipe is illustrated with a beautiful full-colour photograph to get your taste buds going even before you start. If you're just a beginner, you'll find that the comprehensive introduction is packed with invaluable information to get you started, not to mention some useful tips to help you along the way. So now there's no excuse – you have everything you need to start baking!

GETTING STARTED

Choosing bakeware

If you bake regularly, it helps to have a basic selection of cake tins.

- Baking trays – with and without lip

- Deep round and square tins, 18–23 cm/ 7–9 inches

- 2–3 shallow round sandwich tins, 18–20-cm/7–8 inches

- Rectangular traybake tin, about 20 x 30 cm/ 8 x 12 inches

- Round springform tin, 20–23 cm/8–9 inches

- Loaf tins – 450 g/1 lb and 900 g/2 lb

- 12-cup muffin tin

- 12-cup shallow bun tin

- Loose-based tart tin, 20–23 cm/8–9 inches

Fancy tins such as ring tins, Madeleine tins or Bundt tins can be added as required.

Successful baking needs good-quality bakeware that will conduct the heat efficiently and evenly to cake mixtures and will last for years without rusting or warping. Stainless steel tins are long-lasting and will not warp, while aluminium is cheaper but less durable. Non-stick tins can make for easy turning out, but they may not be as durable as uncoated tins. Flexible silicone bakeware is a good alternative to traditional metal tins, but can be expensive.

Why it's important to use the correct tin

If possible, always use the tin size stated in the recipe, as cooking times have been calculated for the stated tin, and if you change it to a very different tin the cake may cook unevenly and give a disappointing result.

What to do if you don't have the correct tin

If you don't have the right tin for the recipe, you don't necessarily have to rush out and buy a new one. Unless it's a particularly unusual shape, most cake tins can be changed for one of the same capacity without harm.

If the recipe uses a round tin but you prefer to use a square one, the square tin should be 2.5 cm/1 inch smaller than the round one. So if the recipe calls for a 23-cm/9-inch round tin, you can substitute a 20-cm/8-inch square one.

GREASING & LINING TINS

Not all cake tins need to be fully lined for baking. For many simple sponges you just need to give the base and sides of the tin a quick brush of oil or melted butter and insert a piece of non-stick baking paper in the base. Richer or low-fat mixtures usually need a thoroughly greased and lined tin to prevent sticking.

Lining a round tin

1 Grease the tin. Cut a strip of baking parchment about 2.5 cm/1 inch longer than the circumference and about 2.5 cm/ 1 inch deeper than the tin.

2 Fold up one long edge about 1 cm/^{1}/$_2$ inch, then unfold leaving a crease.

3 Use scissors to snip cuts along the folded edge of the paper, so that it can be eased into the tin to fit around the curve at the base.

4 Place the tin on a sheet of baking paper and draw around it with a pencil to mark the size. Cut with scissors just inside the line, making a round to fit inside the base, covering the snipped edges of the side lining paper. Grease the paper.

Lining a square tin

1 Grease the tin. Cut a strip of baking parchment about 2.5 cm/1 inch longer than the circumference of the tin and 2.5 cm/ 1 inch deeper.

2 Fold up one long edge about 1 cm/^{1}/$_2$ inch, then unfold leaving a crease. Fit the paper into the sides of the tin, cutting a diagonal slit into the folded edge to fit each corner.

3 Place the tin on a sheet of baking paper, draw around it to mark the size, then cut just inside the line to make a square. Lay the square inside the tin, covering the folded edges. Grease the paper.

Lining a Swiss roll tin or traybake tin

1 Grease the base and sides of the tin. Cut a piece of baking paper 7 cm/2^3/$_4$ inches larger than the tin.

2 Place the tin on the paper, then make a cut from each corner of the paper in towards the tin corner.

3 Place the paper inside the tin so that the diagonally cut corners overlap and fit neatly. Grease the paper.

Lining a loaf tin

1 Grease the tin. Cut a strip of baking paper the length of the tin base and wide enough to cover the base and long sides. Place the paper in the tin.

2 Cut a second piece of parchment the width of the tin base and long enough to cover the base and ends of the tin. Slot this in over the first piece to line the tin, then grease the paper.

Flouring tins

1 Grease the base and sides of the tin, then slip a piece of non-stick baking paper in the base. Grease the paper.

2 Sprinkle a little flour into the tin. Tilt the tin, tapping lightly, so the flour coats the base and sides evenly. Tip out any excess.

ADDITIONAL EQUIPMENT

Oven

A reliable oven is essential to successful baking, and it's a good idea to check yours regularly with an oven thermometer to make sure it's accurate. Preheat the oven to the required temperature for 10–15 minutes before use, so that it has time to fully reach the correct temperature. Fan ovens cook more quickly than conventional ovens, so cooking times can be reduced by 5–10 minutes per hour, or the temperature may be reduced by 10–20°C/50–68°F.

Avoid the temptation to keep opening the oven door to check on your cake, particularly early in the cooking time, as a sudden rush of cold air may cause the cake to sink.

Scales

Many expert cooks can measure ingredients without scales, but for most of us an accurate pair of kitchen scales is essential, particularly for baking. Digital, spring or balance scales are all efficient if used correctly, and most have dual metric and imperial markings or weights. Always follow the same units of measurement throughout – do not mix metric and imperial. Make sure your scales are positioned on a level surface, and weigh out all the ingredients before starting to mix.

Measuring jugs

A heatproof glass or polythene jug is a good choice as it's hard-wearing and easy to clean. Metal and ceramic ones are useful but less easy to use. Choose one with a good pouring lip and clear markings, either metric or imperial. Place the jug on a flat surface at eye level for accurate measuring of liquid ingredients.

Measuring spoons

It's important to use standard measuring spoons, measured level unless stated otherwise, as ordinary kitchen tablespoons and teaspoons can vary in size. In all the recipes in this book, a teaspoon is assumed to hold 5 ml and a tablespoon is assumed to hold 15 ml.

Electric mixer/food processor

A hand-held electric mixer with a powerful motor can be used for creaming, whisking, blending and kneading. Table-top mixers, with greater capacity and more power, are useful for all mixtures, particularly large quantities.

Food processors can cream, blend or knead, as well as doing other cooking tasks. Again, choose one with a powerful motor for durability.

Take care when using a food processor or powerful electric mixer for making cakes as they mix the ingredients very quickly. It is important not to overbeat cake mixtures as this will make them close-textured. Food processors are unsuitable for mixing meringues because the enclosed bowl does not hold enough air to give them volume.

Spoons

Wooden spoons are useful for creaming and mixing. Make sure to keep separate those used for cooking strongly flavoured food, such as onions, as wood can absorb flavours and may transfer them to more delicate mixtures. Heat-resistant nylon spoons are durable and less absorbent of flavours. A large metal spoon is useful for folding in ingredients.

Spatula

You'll find a flexible rubber or silicone spatula helpful for light mixing and scraping out bowls cleanly. Some have a spoon-shaped blade which helps when transferring cake mix from the bowl to the tin.

Bowls

A selection of different-sized mixing bowls is essential, and a set of toughened glass bowls is a good basic start as they are durable, heatproof and easy to clean. Melamine, polythene and ceramic bowls often have pouring lips, and some have non-slip bases to grip the worktop.

Wire cooling racks

A wire rack allows your cakes to cool evenly and prevents condensation, which can cause soggy texture and poor keeping quality. They vary from a simple metal rectangle, to expanding three-tier ones, which are useful for large batches of baking. Some have a non-stick coating for easier cleaning.

Sieve

A good-quality, rustproof metal or nylon sieve is necessary for sifting together dry ingredients evenly, and a set of three sizes is useful. Even nylon ones are hard-wearing and will stand boiling water, but metal ones are the most durable and will last for years.

Graters

A hard-wearing, stainless steel box grater, or flat 'Microplane' type graters with firm grip handles, are good for grating citrus rind, cheese, apple, chocolate, nutmeg etc. You'll need a fine, medium and coarse grater. Some also have a slicing option.

Citrus squeezer/reamer

A sturdy plastic, metal, toughened glass or ceramic squeezer is used for extracting juice from citrus fruits. For smooth juice you'll need one with a filter part to extract all the fibres from the juice. A wooden reamer squeezes out the juice by simply pushing into the halved fruit, but you may also get some pips.

Rolling pin

For rolling pastry and biscuit doughs, a wooden rolling pin is a good tool and you can shape and cool tuiles on it too. Marble, granite or glass rolling pins are more expensive but their cool, smooth surface is good for rolling sticky mixtures.

Pastry brush

A pastry brush is the easiest way to grease cake tins evenly, and can also be used for applying glazes evenly. They are available with natural bristles or more durable synthetic bristles.

Biscuit cutters

A set of round biscuit cutters, with either plain or fluted edges, is a good basic choice, preferably in metal. Later you can add fancy-shaped cutters. Make sure the cutting edge is sharp and the top edge is rolled to safeguard your fingers and keep the cutter rigid.

Piping bag and nozzles

For decorative piping of frostings or soft mixtures, you'll need piping bags and nozzles. Strong nylon or fabric bags are washable and re-usable, or you can buy strong disposable bags to save work. A small selection of stainless steel nozzles should include a plain writing, small and large star and plain large vegetable nozzles.

GLOSSARY OF BAKING TERMS

Baking blind

Baking a pastry-lined flan or tart tin without filling. Place a round of baking paper or greaseproof paper on top of the pastry and fill with dried beans, rice or ceramic baking beans, then bake as the recipe instructs.

Beating

A method of vigorously agitating with a spoon, fork or whisk, to combine ingredients evenly, to soften ingredients, such as butter, or to incorporate air into mixtures.

Creaming

To beat together mixtures of fat and sugar to soften to a pale, fluffy consistency, incorporating air into the mix to make a light, spongy cake, such as a Victoria sponge cake.

Dredging

To sprinkle a mixture or surface generously with a dry ingredient, such as flour or icing sugar, either using a sieve or a 'dredger' pot, which has a top with holes for even sprinkling.

Dusting

To sprinkle a surface lightly with a dry ingredient, such as flour, icing sugar or spices, to give a thin coating, using a fine sieve or dredger to distribute evenly.

Folding in

A method of combining a creamed mixture with dry ingredients, or to incorporate whisked egg whites, so that as little air is knocked out as possible. Ideally, use a large metal spoon to cut and fold the dry ingredients through the mixture, agitating as little as possible to retain air bubbles for lightness.

Glazing

To brush a coating over a mixture either before or after baking, to give a glossy appearance or improve the flavour. For instance, beaten egg or milk are used to glaze pastries and breads, and syrups or jams may be brushed over a cake top for an attractive finish.

Kneading

A process of pressing and stretching a dough, with the hands or a dough hook, to strengthen the gluten (the protein in wheat flour). This makes the gluten more elastic, enabling the dough to rise easily and giving an even texture to the finished product.

Knocking back

This is a second kneading, usually done after the dough has been left to rise and before shaping, with the purpose of knocking out any large air bubbles from the dough, to ensure an even-textured result.

Piping

Forcing a soft cake or biscuit mixture, or an icing or frosting, from a piping bag through a nozzle, usually to create a decorative shape or effect, such as stars, rosettes or lines. Use a firm, even pressure for best results.

Proving

To leave a bread dough to rise after shaping, usually in a warm place. This is done to give the finished bread a good rise and a light, even texture.

Rubbing in

A method of incorporating fat, such as butter, into dry ingredients, such as flour, using the fingertips to rub the two together evenly. The fingertips are the coolest part of the hand, and a cool, light touch helps to give a short texture to pastry, scones and cakes.

Sifting

To shake dry ingredients, such as flour, through a sieve to eliminate lumps and give a smooth texture. It can also help to evenly distribute any added raising agents or spices.

Whipping

A term used to describe the gentle beating of a mixture, usually with a whisk, to make it smooth or incorporate air. For example, it is used to thicken whipping or double cream, or make it stiff enough for piping.

Whisking

Rapidly beating a mixture using a hand whisk or electric whisk to incorporate and trap large amounts of air. This method is used for whisked sponge cakes, which rely totally on air for a light, open texture, and meringues, where the egg whites are whisked until they are stiff enough to hold peaks.

TOP TIPS FOR PERFECT RESULTS

CAKES

The right ingredients

Avoid using low-fat spreads in cakes unless the recipe has been written specially for these, as they have a high moisture content and tend to give a heavy, poor-textured result with traditional recipes. Ordinary 'tub' margarines or spreadable butters have 80 per cent fat content, and these are best for all-in-one creamed mixtures.

Run out of self-raising flour? Make your own by adding $2^1/_2$ teaspoons of baking powder to each 225 g/8 oz plain flour. Sift together thoroughly before use to ensure the raising agent is evenly distributed.

Easy mixing

Allow the butter or margarine to come to room temperature and soften for at least 30 minutes before use, to make it easy to cream.

Always use eggs at room temperature for baking, particularly in whisked mixtures. They will whisk to a larger volume when used at room temperature.

Preventing curdling

When adding eggs to a creamed mixture, always add them gradually at first and beat hard after each addition to prevent curdling. If a cake mixture should start to curdle, quickly beat in a tablespoon or two of flour, which should correct it.

How to tell when a cake is cooked

To check a **sponge cake**, press it lightly on top with your fingertips – it should feel springy to the touch and spring back without leaving an impression.

Most cakes, particularly whisked sponges, will begin to shrink slightly away from the sides of the tin when they are cooked, so this is a good indication.

To test a **rich fruit cake**, remove from the oven and place on the work top, then listen closely to the cake. If you can hear the cake mixture sizzling, it needs more cooking. If you can't hear anything, it should be cooked.

The skewer test is also a useful check – insert a skewer into the centre of the cake then withdraw it quickly; if there is a residue of sticky mixture on the skewer then the cake needs more cooking. If it comes out clean, the cake is cooked.

Successful storage

Make sure that your cakes and bakes are completely cooled before storing, as any residual warmth may cause condensation that will result in mould developing on the cake.

Rich fruit cakes should store for months and will improve with keeping. Wrap closely in a double layer of greaseproof paper then overwrap with foil or a polythene bag. Store in a cool, dry place with an even temperature.

PASTRY

Shortcrust pastry

Make sure all your ingredients and utensils are really cold, as this helps to make a really light, crisp pastry.

Once the liquid has been added, handle the pastry as lightly and as little as possible, or it will be difficult to handle and will become heavy when baked.

If possible, chill the pastry after shaping to prevent shrinkage during cooking.

Flaky or puff pastry

Before baking, dampen the baking tray with a water spray or rinse under the tap; the water will turn to steam that will help the pastry rise.

When glazing puff or flaky pastry, take care to avoid brushing over the cut edges as this can spoil the rise.

Choux pastry

It's important to beat the mixture thoroughly after adding the eggs to incorporate as much air as possible for a really light pastry. You can use a hand mixer for this.

Choux pastry freezes well raw, so choux pastry balls can be piped onto a baking tray and frozen. Thaw completely before baking as in the recipe.

Filo pastry

To prevent sheets of filo pastry drying out while you work, cover them with a sheet of clingfilm then with a lightly dampened tea towel. Avoid the damp tea towel coming in contact with the pastry as this will cause it to stick.

If possible, fillings for filo pastry should be cooled before use, as warm mixtures may cause the pastry to soften and make it difficult to shape.

Lining a tart tin or pie plate

1 Place the tart tin or pie plate on a baking tray. Roll out the pastry to a round about 5 cm/ 2 inches larger than the tin.

2 Carefully roll the pastry over the rolling pin and lift over the tin, then unroll it evenly without stretching.

3 Carefully ease the pastry into the sides of the tin, using your fingertips to press right into the edges to fit the shape closely without an air gap.

4 Roll a rolling pin over the top of the tin to trim off the surplus pastry. Alternatively, for a plain tart tin or pie plate, trim with a knife, then pinch the edges with your fingers for a fluted edge.

Baking blind

This is a method of part-baking pastry for flans and tarts before adding the filling to ensure crisp, evenly cooked pastry that doesn't rise up underneath.

1 Roll out the pastry and use it to line the tart tin, trimming the top edge by rolling a rolling pin over the top. Prick the base all over with a fork.

2 Cut a piece of baking paper about 7 cm/ 2³/₄ inches larger than the tin and place it inside the pastry-lined case.

3 Half-fill the paper with dried beans or ceramic baking beans to weigh the pastry down as it cooks.

4 Bake the pastry as in the recipe, usually for about 10 minutes, then remove the paper and beans and bake for a further 5 minutes to dry out before adding the filling.

BISCUITS

When making biscuits from a soft mixture that will spread, allow at least 7 cm/2³/₄ inches between each one when placing the mix on the baking sheet, to prevent the biscuits joining together as they bake.

To stamp out biscuits cleanly with a biscuit cutter, rub the edges of the cutter into flour to prevent the biscuit dough from sticking to the cutter.

When making biscuits from a rolled-out dough, it's worth making a double quantity and freezing half – roll it into a sausage shape, overwrap with foil and freeze for up to three months. To use, thaw for about an hour at room temperature then slice and bake as usual.

To add extra fibre and texture to plain biscuits, roll out on a surface dusted with oatmeal or bran instead of flour.

BREAD

Tips on baking with yeast

To ensure the water is at the correct temperature for the yeast, mix one third boiling water with two thirds cold water. It should feel tepid, i.e. neither cold nor hot to the touch.

When using easy-blend (fast-action) yeast, make sure you add it to the dry ingredients first, never mix with liquid as with conventional yeast. Follow the pack directions.

A cooked loaf sounds hollow when tapped underneath – tap it firmly on the base with your knuckles to check.

Kneading dough

There are several methods of kneading dough, but this is a useful basic method for most types of dough:

1 Turn out the dough onto a lightly floured work surface. Fold the dough in half towards you, then use the heel of your hand to push it firmly down and away from you.

2 Give the dough a quarter turn, then repeat the folding and pushing action constantly for about 5 minutes, until the dough is smooth and no longer sticky.

Alternatively, use a dough hook on an electric mixer or food processor; you'll need a mixer with a powerful motor for large batches of dough.

EVERYDAY CAKES

VICTORIA SPONGE CAKE

Preheat the oven to 180°C/350°F/Gas Mark 4. Grease and line the bases of two 20-cm/8-inch sandwich tins.

Sift the flour and baking powder into a bowl and add the butter, sugar and eggs. Mix together, then beat well until smooth.

Divide the mixture evenly between the prepared tins and smooth the surfaces. Bake in the preheated oven for 25–30 minutes, or until well risen and golden brown, and the cakes feel springy when lightly pressed.

Leave to cool in the tins for 5 minutes, then turn out and peel off the lining paper. Transfer to wire racks to cool completely. Sandwich the cakes together with the raspberry jam, whipped double cream and strawberry halves. Dust with icing sugar and serve.

SERVES 8

175 g/6 oz self-raising flour

1 tsp baking powder

175 g/6 oz butter, softened,
   plus extra for greasing

175 g/6 oz golden caster sugar

3 eggs

icing sugar, for dusting

filling

3 tbsp raspberry jam

300 ml/10 fl oz double cream,
   whipped

16 fresh strawberries, halved

CHOCOLATE FUDGE CAKE

Preheat the oven to 180°C/350°F/Gas Mark 4. Grease and line the bases of two 20-cm/8-inch sandwich tins.

To make the icing, place the chocolate, muscovado sugar, butter, evaporated milk and vanilla extract in a heavy-based saucepan. Heat gently, stirring constantly, until melted. Pour into a bowl and leave to cool. Cover and chill in the refrigerator for 1 hour, or until spreadable.

For the cake, place the butter and caster sugar in a bowl and beat together until light and fluffy. Gradually beat in the eggs. Stir in the golden syrup and ground almonds. Sift the flour, salt and cocoa powder into a separate bowl, then fold into the mixture. Add a little water, if necessary, to make a dropping consistency.

Spoon the mixture into the prepared tins and bake in the preheated oven for 30–35 minutes, or until springy to the touch and a skewer inserted in the centre comes out clean.

Leave the cakes in the tins for 5 minutes, then turn out onto wire racks to cool completely. When the cakes are cold, sandwich them together with half the icing. Spread the remaining icing over the top and sides of the cake, swirling it to give a frosted appearance.

SERVES 8

175 g/6 oz unsalted butter, softened, plus extra for greasing

175 g/6 oz golden caster sugar

3 eggs, beaten

3 tbsp golden syrup

40 g/1½ oz ground almonds

175 g/6 oz self-raising flour

pinch of salt

40 g/1½ oz cocoa powder

icing

225 g/8 oz plain chocolate, broken into pieces

55 g/2 oz dark muscovado sugar

225 g/8 oz unsalted butter, diced

5 tbsp evaporated milk

½ tsp vanilla extract

COFFEE & WALNUT CAKE

SERVES 8

175 g/6 oz unsalted butter,
  plus extra for greasing

175 g/6 oz light muscovado sugar

3 large eggs, beaten

3 tbsp strong black coffee

175 g/6 oz self-raising flour

1½ tsp baking powder

115 g/4 oz walnut pieces

walnut halves, to decorate

frosting

115 g/4 oz unsalted butter

200 g/7 oz icing sugar

1 tbsp strong black coffee

½ tsp vanilla extract

Preheat the oven to 180°C/350°F/Gas Mark 4. Grease and line the bases of two 20-cm/8-inch sandwich tins.

Cream together the butter and muscovado sugar until pale and fluffy. Gradually add the eggs, beating well after each addition. Beat in the coffee.

Sift the flour and baking powder into the mixture, then fold in lightly and evenly with a metal spoon. Fold in the walnut pieces.

Divide the mixture between the prepared cake tins and smooth level. Bake in the preheated oven for 20–25 minutes, or until golden brown and springy to the touch. Turn out onto a wire rack to cool.

For the frosting, beat together the butter, icing sugar, coffee and vanilla extract, mixing until smooth and creamy.

Use about half the mixture to sandwich the cakes together, then spread the remaining frosting on top and swirl with a palette knife. Decorate with walnut halves.

STICKY TOFFEE
CAKE

Preheat the oven to 180°C/350°F/Gas Mark 4. Grease and line a 20-cm/8-inch square cake tin.

Put the dates in a small saucepan with the boiling water and bicarbonate of soda. Heat gently for about 5 minutes, without boiling, until the dates are soft.

Cream together the butter and caster sugar in a bowl until light and fluffy. Beat in the egg, vanilla extract and date mixture.

Fold in the flour using a metal spoon, mixing evenly. Pour the mixture into the prepared cake tin. Bake in the preheated oven for 40–45 minutes, or until firm to the touch and just starting to shrink away from the sides of the tin.

For the toffee sauce, combine the muscovado sugar, butter and cream in a saucepan and heat gently until the sugar has dissolved. Simmer gently, stirring, for about 2 minutes.

Remove the cake from the oven and prick all over the surface with a skewer or fork. Pour the hot toffee sauce evenly over the surface. Leave it to cool in the tin, then cut into squares.

SERVES 9

175 g/6 oz stoned dates, chopped

175 ml/6 fl oz boiling water

½ tsp bicarbonate of soda

85 g/3 oz butter, plus extra
   for greasing

140 g/5 oz caster sugar

1 large egg, beaten

½ tsp vanilla extract

175 g/6 oz self-raising flour

toffee sauce

85 g/3 oz light muscovado sugar

40 g/1½ oz butter

2 tbsp single cream or milk

MADEIRA
CAKE

Preheat the oven to 160°C/325°F/Gas Mark 3. Grease and line an 18-cm/7-inch round deep cake tin.

Cream together the butter and sugar until pale and fluffy. Add the lemon rind and gradually beat in the eggs. Sift in the flours and fold in evenly, adding enough brandy to make a soft dropping consistency.

Spoon the mixture into the prepared tin and smooth the surface. Lay the slices of citron peel on top of the cake.

Bake in the preheated oven for 1–1 ¼ hours, or until well risen, golden brown and springy to the touch.

Cool in the tin for 10 minutes, then turn out and cool completely on a wire rack.

SERVES 8–10

175 g/6 oz unsalted butter, plus extra for greasing

175 g/6 oz caster sugar

finely grated rind of 1 lemon

3 large eggs, beaten

115 g/4 oz plain flour

115 g/4 oz self-raising flour

2–3 tbsp brandy or milk

2 slices of citron peel

CLASSIC CHERRY CAKE

SERVES 8

250 g/9 oz glacé cherries, quartered

85 g/3 oz ground almonds

200 g/7 oz plain flour

1 tsp baking powder

200 g/7 oz unsalted butter, plus extra for greasing

200 g/7 oz caster sugar

3 large eggs

finely grated rind and juice of 1 lemon

6 sugar cubes, crushed

Preheat the oven to 180°C/350°F/Gas Mark 4. Grease a 20-cm/8-inch round cake tin and line the base and sides with non-stick baking paper.

Stir together the cherries, ground almonds and 1 tablespoon of the flour. Sift the remaining flour into a separate bowl with the baking powder.

Cream together the butter and sugar until light in colour and fluffy in texture. Gradually add the eggs, beating hard with each addition, until evenly mixed.

Add the flour mixture and fold lightly and evenly into the creamed mixture with a metal spoon. Add the cherry mixture and fold in evenly. Finally, fold in the lemon rind and juice.

Spoon the mixture into the prepared cake tin and sprinkle with the crushed sugar cubes. Bake in the preheated oven for 1–1¼ hours, or until risen, golden brown and the cake is just beginning to shrink away from the sides of the tin.

Cool in the tin for about 15 minutes, then turn out to finish cooling on a wire rack.

FROSTED CARROT CAKE

Preheat the oven to 180°C/350°F/Gas Mark 4. Grease and line the base of a 23-cm/9-inch square cake tin.

In a large bowl beat together the oil, muscovado sugar and eggs. Stir in the grated carrots, sultanas, walnuts and orange rind.

Sift together the flour, bicarbonate of soda, cinnamon and nutmeg, then stir evenly into the carrot mixture.

Spoon the mixture into the prepared cake tin and bake in the preheated oven for 40–45 minutes, until well risen and firm to the touch.

Remove the cake from the oven and set on a wire rack for 5 minutes. Turn out onto a wire rack to cool completely.

For the frosting, combine the soft cheese, icing sugar and orange juice in a bowl and beat until smooth. Spread over the top of the cake and swirl with a palette knife. Decorate with strips of orange zest and serve cut into squares.

SERVES 16

175 ml/6 fl oz sunflower oil, plus extra for greasing

175 g/6 oz light muscovado sugar

3 eggs, beaten

175 g/6 oz grated carrots

85 g/3 oz sultanas

55 g/2 oz walnut pieces

grated rind of 1 orange

175 g/6 oz self-raising flour

1 tsp bicarbonate of soda

1 tsp ground cinnamon

½ tsp grated nutmeg

strips of orange zest, to decorate

frosting

200 g/7 oz full-fat soft cheese

100 g/3½ oz icing sugar

2 tsp orange juice

GINGERBREAD

Preheat the oven to 180°C/350°F/Gas Mark 4. Grease a 23-cm/ 9-inch square deep cake tin and line the base with non-stick baking paper.

Place the butter, sugar and golden syrup in a saucepan and heat gently, stirring until melted. Remove from the heat.

Beat in the orange rind and juice, eggs, flours and ground ginger, then beat thoroughly to mix evenly. Stir in the glacé ginger.

Spoon the batter into the prepared tin and bake in the preheated oven for 40–45 minutes, or until risen and firm to the touch.

Cool in the tin for about 10 minutes, then turn out and finish cooling on a wire rack. Cut into squares and decorate with some glacé ginger.

SERVES 9

175 g/6 oz unsalted butter, plus extra for greasing

150 g/5½ oz dark muscovado sugar

175 g/6 oz golden syrup

finely grated rind and juice of 1 small orange

2 large eggs, beaten

225 g/8 oz self-raising flour

100 g/3½ oz plain wholemeal flour

2 tsp ground ginger

40 g/1½ oz chopped glacé ginger or stem ginger

pieces of glacé ginger or stem ginger, to decorate

CARIBBEAN COCONUT CAKE

SERVES 10

280 g/10 oz butter, softened,
  plus extra for greasing

175 g/6 oz golden caster sugar

3 eggs

175 g/6 oz self-raising flour

1½ tsp baking powder

½ tsp freshly grated nutmeg

55 g/2 oz desiccated coconut

5 tbsp coconut cream

280 g/10 oz icing sugar

5 tbsp pineapple jam

toasted desiccated coconut,
  to decorate

Preheat the oven to 180ºC/350ºF/Gas Mark 4. Grease and line the bases of two 20-cm/8-inch sandwich tins.

Place 175 g/6 oz of the butter in a bowl with the caster sugar and eggs and sift in the flour, baking powder and nutmeg. Beat together until smooth, then stir in the desiccated coconut and 2 tablespoons of the coconut cream.

Divide the mixture between the prepared tins and smooth the tops. Bake in the preheated oven for 25 minutes, or until golden and firm to the touch. Leave to cool in the tins for 5 minutes, then turn out onto a wire rack, peel off the lining paper and leave to cool completely.

Sift the icing sugar into a bowl and add the remaining butter and coconut cream. Beat together until smooth. Spread the pineapple jam on one of the cakes and top with just under half of the buttercream. Place the other cake on top. Spread the remaining buttercream on top of the cake and scatter with toasted desiccated coconut.

DEVIL'S FOOD CAKE

Preheat the oven to 160°C/325°F/Gas Mark 3. Grease two 20-cm/ 8-inch sandwich tins and line the bases with non-stick baking paper.

Break up the chocolate and place with the milk and cocoa powder in a heatproof bowl over a saucepan of hot water, then heat gently, stirring, until melted and smooth. Remove from the heat.

In a large bowl beat together the butter and muscovado sugar until pale and fluffy. Beat in the egg yolks, then the soured cream and the melted chocolate mixture. Sift in the flour and bicarbonate of soda, then fold in evenly. In a separate bowl, whisk the egg whites until stiff enough to hold firm peaks. Fold into the mixture lightly and evenly.

Divide the mixture between the prepared cake tins, smooth level and bake in the preheated oven for 35–40 minutes, or until risen and firm to the touch. Cool in the tins for 10 minutes, then turn out onto a wire rack.

For the frosting, place the chocolate, cocoa powder, soured cream, golden syrup, butter and water in a saucepan and heat gently, until melted. Remove from the heat and sift in the icing sugar, stirring until smooth. Cool, stirring occasionally, until the mixture begins to thicken and hold its shape.

Split the cakes in half horizontally with a sharp knife, to make four layers. Sandwich the cakes together with about a third of the frosting. Spread the remainder over the top and sides of the cakes, swirling with a palette knife.

SERVES 8–10

140 g/5 oz plain chocolate

100 ml/3½ fl oz milk

2 tbsp cocoa powder

140 g/5 oz unsalted butter, plus extra for greasing

140 g/5 oz light muscovado sugar

3 eggs, separated

4 tbsp soured cream or crème fraîche

200 g/7 oz plain flour

1 tsp bicarbonate of soda

frosting

140 g/5 oz plain chocolate

40 g/1½ oz cocoa powder

4 tbsp soured cream or crème fraîche

1 tbsp golden syrup

40 g/1½ oz unsalted butter

4 tbsp water

200 g/7 oz icing sugar

ANGEL FOOD CAKE

Preheat the oven to 160°C/325°F/Gas Mark 3. Brush the inside of a 1.7-litre/3-pint ring tin with oil and dust lightly with flour.

In a clean, grease-free bowl, whisk the egg whites until they hold soft peaks. Add the cream of tartar and whisk again until the whites are stiff but not dry.

Whisk in the almond extract, then add the sugar, a tablespoon at a time, whisking hard between each addition. Sift in the flour and fold in lightly and evenly using a large metal spoon.

Spoon the mixture into the prepared cake tin and tap on the work surface to remove any large air bubbles. Bake in the preheated oven for 40–45 minutes, or until golden brown and firm to the touch.

Run the tip of a small knife around the edges of the cake to loosen from the tin. Leave to cool in the tin for 10 minutes, then turn out onto a wire rack to finish cooling.

To serve, place the berries, lemon juice and icing sugar in a saucepan and heat gently until the sugar has dissolved. Serve with the cake.

SERVES 10

sunflower oil, for greasing

8 large egg whites

1 tsp cream of tartar

1 tsp almond extract

250 g/9 oz caster sugar

115 g/4 oz plain flour, plus extra for dusting

to serve

250 g/9 oz summer berries

1 tbsp lemon juice

2 tbsp icing sugar

RICH FRUIT CAKE

SERVES 16

350 g/12 oz sultanas

225 g/8 oz raisins

115 g/4 oz ready-to-eat dried
    apricots, chopped

85 g/3 oz stoned dates, chopped

4 tbsp dark rum or brandy, plus
    extra for flavouring (optional)

finely grated rind and juice of
    1 orange

225 g/8 oz unsalted butter, plus
    extra for greasing

225 g/8 oz light muscovado sugar

4 eggs

70 g/2½ oz chopped mixed peel

85 g/3 oz glacé cherries,
    quartered

25 g/1 oz chopped glacé ginger or
    stem ginger

40 g/1½ oz blanched almonds,
    chopped

200 g/7 oz plain flour

1 tsp ground mixed spice

Place the sultanas, raisins, apricots and dates in a large bowl and stir in the rum, orange rind and orange juice. Cover and leave to soak for several hours or overnight.

Preheat the oven to 150°C/300°F/Gas Mark 2. Grease and line a 20-cm/8-inch round deep cake tin.

Cream together the butter and sugar until light and fluffy. Gradually beat in the eggs, beating hard after each addition. Stir in the soaked fruits, mixed peel, glacé cherries, glacé ginger and blanched almonds.

Sift together the flour and mixed spice, then fold lightly and evenly into the mixture. Spoon the mixture into the prepared cake tin and level the surface, making a slight depression in the centre with the back of the spoon.

Bake in the preheated oven for 2¼–2¾ hours, or until the cake is beginning to shrink away from the sides and a skewer inserted into the centre comes out clean. Cool completely in the tin.

Turn out the cake and remove the lining paper. Wrap in greaseproof paper and foil, and store for at least two months before use. To add a richer flavour, prick the cake with a skewer and spoon over a couple of extra tablespoons of rum or brandy, if using, before storing.

CRISPY-TOPPED FRUIT BAKE

Preheat the oven to 190°C/375°F/Gas Mark 5. Grease and line a 900-g/2-lb loaf tin.

Peel, core and finely dice the apples. Place them in a saucepan with the lemon juice, bring to the boil, cover and simmer for about 10 minutes, until soft and pulpy. Beat well and set aside to cool.

Sift the flour, baking powder and cinnamon into a bowl, adding any husks that remain in the sieve. Stir in 70 g/2½ oz of the blackberries and the sugar.

Make a well in the centre of the ingredients and add the egg, yogurt and cooled apple purée. Mix well to incorporate thoroughly. Spoon the mixture into the prepared tin and smooth the top.

Sprinkle with the remaining blackberries, pressing them down into the cake mixture, and top with the crushed sugar lumps. Bake in the preheated oven for 40–45 minutes. Remove from the oven and set aside in the tin to cool.

Remove the cake from the tin and peel away the lining paper. Serve dusted with cinnamon.

SERVES 10

butter, for greasing

350 g/12 oz cooking apples

3 tbsp lemon juice

350 g/12 oz self-raising wholemeal flour

½ tsp baking powder

1 tsp ground cinnamon, plus extra for dusting

115 g/4 oz prepared blackberries, thawed, if frozen

115 g/4 oz light muscovado sugar

1 egg, beaten

200 ml/7 fl oz low-fat natural yogurt

55 g/2 oz white or brown sugar lumps, lightly crushed

CHOCOLATE & VANILLA MARBLED LOAF

Preheat the oven to 160°C/325°F/Gas Mark 3. Grease a 450-g/ 1-lb loaf tin and line the base with non-stick baking paper. Dust a little flour around the inside of the tin, shaking out the excess.

Break up the chocolate, place in a small heatproof bowl with the milk and set over a saucepan of simmering water. Heat gently until just melted. Remove from the heat.

Cream together the butter and sugar until light and fluffy. Beat in the egg and soured cream. Sift the flour and baking powder over the mixture, then fold in lightly and evenly using a metal spoon.

Spoon half the mixture into a separate bowl and stir in the chocolate mixture. Add the vanilla extract to the plain mixture.

Spoon the chocolate and vanilla mixtures alternately into the prepared loaf tin, swirling lightly with a knife or skewer for a marbled effect. Bake in the preheated oven for 40–45 minutes, or until well-risen and firm to the touch.

Cool in the tin for 10 minutes, then turn out and finish cooling on a wire rack.

SERVES 8

55 g/2 oz plain chocolate

3 tbsp milk

70 g/2½ oz unsalted butter, plus extra for greasing

85 g/3 oz caster sugar

1 egg, beaten

3 tbsp soured cream

115 g/4 oz self-raising flour, plus extra for dusting

½ tsp baking powder

½ tsp vanilla extract

BANANA LOAF

SERVES 8

butter, for greasing

125 g/4½ oz white self-raising
  flour

100 g/3½ oz light brown
  self-raising flour

150 g/5½ oz demerara sugar

pinch of salt

½ tsp ground cinnamon

½ tsp ground nutmeg

2 large ripe bananas, peeled

175 ml/6 fl oz orange juice

2 eggs, beaten

4 tbsp rapeseed oil

Preheat the oven to 180ºC/350ºF/Gas Mark 4. Lightly grease and line a 900-g/2-lb loaf tin.

Sift the flours, sugar, salt and the spices into a large bowl. In a separate bowl mash the bananas with the orange juice, then stir in the eggs and oil. Pour into the dry ingredients and mix well.

Spoon into the prepared tin and bake in the preheated oven for 1 hour. Test to see if the loaf is cooked by inserting a skewer into the centre. If it comes out clean, the loaf is done. If not, bake for a further 10 minutes and test again.

Remove from the oven and leave to cool in the tin. Turn out the loaf, slice and serve.

DATE & WALNUT TEABREAD

Preheat the oven to 180°C/350°F/Gas Mark 4. Grease a 450-g/1-lb loaf tin and line the base with non-stick baking paper.

Place the dates, bicarbonate of soda and lemon rind in a bowl and add the hot tea. Leave to soak for 10 minutes, until soft.

Cream together the butter and sugar until light and fluffy, then beat in the egg. Stir in the date mixture.

Fold in the flour using a large metal spoon, then fold in the walnuts. Spoon the mixture into the prepared cake tin and spread evenly. Top with walnut halves.

Bake in the preheated oven for 35–40 minutes, or until risen, firm and golden brown. Cool for 10 minutes in the tin, then turn out the loaf and finish cooling on a wire rack.

SERVES 8

100 g/3½ oz stoned dates, chopped

½ tsp bicarbonate of soda

finely grated rind of ½ lemon

100 ml/3½ fl oz hot tea

40 g/1½ oz unsalted butter, plus extra for greasing

70 g/2½ oz light muscovado sugar

1 small egg

125 g/4½ oz self-raising flour

25 g/1 oz walnuts, chopped

walnut halves, to decorate

GLOSSY FRUIT LOAF

Place the raisins, apricots and dates in a bowl, pour over the tea and leave to soak for 8 hours, or overnight.

Preheat the oven to 160ºC/325ºF/Gas Mark 3. Grease and line a 900-g/2-lb loaf tin.

Beat the butter and sugar together until light and fluffy. Gradually beat in the eggs, then fold in the flour alternately with the soaked fruit. Gently stir in the glacé pineapple, glacé cherries and chopped Brazil nuts. Spoon the mixture into the prepared tin. For the topping, arrange the walnut halves, whole Brazil nuts and glacé cherries over the surface.

Bake in the preheated oven for 1½–1¾ hours, or until a skewer inserted into the centre comes out clean. Leave to cool in the tin for 10 minutes, then turn out and peel off the lining paper. Transfer to a wire rack to cool completely. Warm the apricot jam and brush over the top of the cake.

SERVES 10

55 g/2 oz raisins

85 g/3 oz dried apricots, roughly chopped

55 g/2 oz stoned dates, chopped

90 ml/3 fl oz cold black tea

115 g/4 oz butter, plus extra for greasing

115 g/4 oz light muscovado sugar

2 eggs, beaten

175 g/6 oz self-raising flour, sifted

55 g/2 oz glacé pineapple, roughly chopped

85 g/3 oz glacé cherries, halved

85 g/3 oz Brazil nuts, roughly chopped

topping

walnut halves

whole Brazil nuts

glacé cherries, halved

2 tbsp apricot jam, sieved

BATTENBERG CAKE

SERVES 6–8

115 g/4 oz butter or margarine, softened, plus extra for greasing

115 g/4 oz caster sugar, plus extra for sprinkling

2 eggs, lightly beaten

1 tsp vanilla extract

115 g/4 oz self-raising flour, sifted

a few drops of pink edible food colouring

2–3 tbsp apricot jam

300 g/10½ oz marzipan

Preheat the oven to 180°C/350°F/Gas Mark 4. Grease and line an 18-cm/7-inch shallow square baking tin. Cut a strip of double baking paper and grease it. Use this to divide the tin in half.

Cream the butter and sugar in a mixing bowl until pale and fluffy. Gently beat in the eggs and vanilla extract, gradually adding in the flour. Spoon half the mixture into a separate bowl and colour it with a few drops of food colouring.

Spoon the plain mixture into half the prepared baking tin. Spoon the coloured mixture into the other half of the tin, trying to make the divide as straight as possible. Bake in the preheated oven for 35–40 minutes. Turn out and leave to cool on a wire rack.

When cool, trim the edges and cut the cake portions lengthways in half, making four equal parts. Warm the jam in a small saucepan. Brush two sides of each cake portion with some of the jam and stick them together to give a chequerboard effect.

Knead the marzipan with a few drops of food colouring to colour it a subtle shade of pink. Roll out the marzipan to a rectangle wide enough to wrap around the cake. Brush the outside of the cake with the remaining jam. Place the cake on the marzipan and wrap the marzipan around the cake, making sure that the seam is on one corner of the cake. Trim the edges neatly. Crimp the top edges of the cake, if desired, and sprinkle with sugar.

LEMON POLENTA CAKE

Preheat the oven to 180°C/350°F/Gas Mark 4. Lightly grease a 20-cm/8-inch round deep cake tin and line the base with baking paper.

Beat together the butter and sugar until pale and fluffy. Beat in the lemon rind, lemon juice, eggs and ground almonds. Sift in the polenta and baking powder and stir until evenly mixed.

Spoon the mixture into the prepared tin and spread evenly. Bake in the preheated oven for 30–35 minutes, or until just firm to the touch and golden brown. Remove the cake from the oven and leave to cool in the tin for 20 minutes.

For the syrup, place the lemon juice, sugar and water in a small saucepan. Heat gently, stirring until the sugar has dissolved, then bring to the boil and simmer for 3–4 minutes, or until slightly reduced and syrupy.

Turn out the cake onto a wire cooling rack then drizzle half of the syrup evenly over the surface. Leave to cool completely.

Cut the cake into slices, drizzle the extra syrup over the top and serve with crème fraîche.

SERVES 8

200 g/7 oz unsalted butter, plus extra for greasing

200 g/7 oz caster sugar

finely grated rind and juice of 1 large lemon

3 eggs, beaten

140 g/5 oz ground almonds

100 g/3½ oz quick-cook polenta

1 tsp baking powder

crème fraîche, to serve

syrup

juice of 2 lemons

55 g/2 oz caster sugar

2 tbsp water

APPLE CAKE WITH STREUSEL TOPPING

Preheat the oven to 180°C/350°F/Gas Mark 4. Grease a 20-cm/ 8-inch round loose-based cake tin and line the base with baking paper. Toss the apples in the lemon juice.

Cream together the butter and caster sugar until pale and fluffy, then gradually add the eggs, beating thoroughly after each addition. Sift together the flour, baking powder, cinnamon and nutmeg into the mixture and fold in lightly and evenly using a metal spoon. Stir in the cider.

Stir the apples into the mixture to distribute evenly, then spoon into the prepared tin and level the surface.

For the streusel topping, mix together the hazelnuts, flour, muscovado sugar and cinnamon, then stir in the melted butter, mixing until crumbly. Spread over the cake.

Bake the cake in the preheated oven for 1–1¼ hours, or until firm and golden brown. Cool for 10 minutes in the tin, then remove carefully and finish cooling on a wire rack.

SERVES 8

500 g/1 lb 2 oz eating apples, peeled, cored and cut into 1-cm/½-inch dice

1 tbsp lemon juice

125 g/4½ oz unsalted butter, plus extra for greasing

125 g/4½ oz golden caster sugar

2 large eggs, beaten

225 g/8 oz plain flour

3 tsp baking powder

1 tsp ground cinnamon

½ tsp ground nutmeg

3 tbsp cider or apple juice

streusel topping

40 g/1½ oz hazelnuts, skinned and finely chopped

40 g/1½ oz plain flour

25 g/1 oz light muscovado sugar

½ tsp ground cinnamon

25 g/1 oz unsalted butter, melted

HONEY & ALMOND CAKE

SERVES 12–16

150 g/5½ oz unsalted butter,
  plus extra for greasing

115 g/4 oz light muscovado sugar

175 g/6 oz clear honey

1 tbsp lemon juice

2 eggs, beaten

200 g/7 oz self-raising flour

15 g/½ oz flaked almonds

warmed honey, to glaze

Preheat the oven to 180°C/350°F/Gas Mark 4. Grease a 20-cm/8-inch square deep cake tin and line the base with baking paper.

Place the butter, sugar, honey and lemon juice in a saucepan and stir over a medium heat, without boiling, until melted and smooth. Remove the pan from the heat and quickly beat in the eggs with a wooden spoon. Sift in the flour and stir lightly and evenly with a metal spoon.

Pour the mixture into the prepared tin and scatter the flaked almonds over the top. Bake in the preheated oven for 35–40 minutes, until risen, firm and golden brown.

Leave the cake to cool in the tin for about 15 minutes, then turn out and cool completely on a wire rack. Brush with the warmed honey and cut into slices to serve.

PINEAPPLE UPSIDE-DOWN CAKE

Preheat the oven to 160°C/325°F/Gas Mark 3. Grease a 23-cm/ 9-inch round deep tin with a solid base and line the base with baking paper.

For the topping, place the butter and golden syrup in a heavy-based saucepan and heat gently until melted. Bring to the boil and boil for 2–3 minutes, stirring, until slightly thickened and toffee-like.

Pour the syrup into the base of the prepared tin. Arrange the pineapple rings and glacé cherries in one layer over the syrup.

Place the eggs, sugar and vanilla extract in a large heatproof bowl over a saucepan of gently simmering water and whisk with an electric mixer for about 10–15 minutes, until thick enough to leave a trail when the whisk is lifted. Sift in the flour and baking powder and fold in lightly and evenly with a metal spoon.

Fold the melted butter into the mixture with a metal spoon until evenly mixed. Spoon into the prepared tin and bake in the preheated oven for 1–1¼ hours, or until well risen, firm and golden brown.

Leave to cool in the tin for 10 minutes, then carefully turn out onto a serving plate. Serve warm or cold.

SERVES 10

4 eggs, beaten

200 g/7 oz golden caster sugar

1 tsp vanilla extract

200 g/7 oz plain flour

2 tsp baking powder

125 g/4½ oz unsalted butter, melted, plus extra for greasing

topping

40 g/1½ oz unsalted butter

4 tbsp golden syrup

425 g/15 oz canned pineapple rings, drained

4–6 glacé cherries, halved

ORANGE & POPPY SEED BUNDT CAKE

Preheat the oven to 160°C/325°F/Gas Mark 3. Grease and lightly flour a Bundt ring tin, about 24 cm/9 inches in diameter and with a capacity of approximately 2 litres/3 pints.

Cream together the butter and sugar until pale and fluffy, then add the eggs gradually, beating thoroughly after each addition. Stir in the orange rind and poppy seeds. Sift in the flour and baking powder, then fold in evenly. Add the milk and orange juice, stirring to mix evenly.

Spoon the mixture into the prepared tin and bake in the preheated oven for 45–50 minutes, or until firm and golden brown. Leave to cool in the tin for 10 minutes, then turn out onto a wire rack to cool.

For the syrup, place the sugar and orange juice in a saucepan and heat gently until the sugar melts. Bring to the boil and simmer for about 5 minutes, until reduced and syrupy.

Spoon the syrup over the cake whilst it is still warm. Top with the strips of orange zest and serve warm or cold.

SERVES 10

200 g/7 oz unsalted butter, plus extra for greasing

200 g/7 oz golden caster sugar

3 large eggs, beaten

finely grated rind of 1 orange

55 g/2 oz poppy seeds

300 g/10½ oz plain flour, plus extra for dusting

2 tsp baking powder

150 ml/5 fl oz milk

125 ml/4 fl oz orange juice

strips of orange zest, to decorate

syrup

140 g/5 oz golden caster sugar

150 ml/5 fl oz orange juice

CELEBRATION CAKES

BIRTHDAY LEMON SPONGE CAKE

Preheat the oven to 180°C/350°C/Gas Mark 4. Grease two 20-cm/8-inch sandwich tins and line the bases with baking paper.

Cream together the butter and caster sugar until pale and fluffy. Gradually add the eggs, beating well after each addition. Sift in the flour and fold in evenly with a metal spoon. Fold in the lemon rind and milk lightly and evenly.

Spoon the mixture into the prepared tins and bake in the preheated oven for 25–30 minutes, or until golden brown and springy to the touch. Leave the cakes to cool in the tins for 2–3 minutes, then turn out onto a wire rack to finish cooling.

For the butter icing, beat together the butter, icing sugar and lemon juice until smooth. Mix about 3 tablespoons of the butter cream with the lemon curd. Use the lemon curd mixture to sandwich the two cakes together.

Spread about two thirds of the remaining butter icing over the top of the cake, swirling with a palette knife. Spoon the remainder into a piping bag and pipe swirls around the edge of the cake. Add candleholders and birthday candles to finish.

SERVES 8–10

250 g/9 oz unsalted butter, plus extra for greasing

250 g/9 oz golden caster sugar

4 eggs, beaten

250 g/9 oz self-raising flour

finely grated rind of 1 lemon

3 tbsp milk

butter icing

140 g/5 oz unsalted butter

200 g/7 oz icing sugar

2 tbsp lemon juice or lemon liqueur (Limoncello)

3 tbsp lemon curd

DOTTY CHOCOLATE CHIP CAKE

Preheat the oven to 170°C/325°F/Gas Mark 3. Grease a 20-cm/ 8-inch round cake tin and line the base with baking paper.

Place the margarine, sugar, eggs, flour, baking powder and cocoa powder in a bowl and beat until just smooth. Stir in the chocolate chips, mixing evenly.

Spoon the mixture into the prepared tin and spread the top level. Bake in the preheated oven for 40–45 minutes, until risen and firm to the touch. Leave to cool in the tin for 5 minutes, then turn out and finish cooling completely on a wire rack.

For the icing, place the chocolate, butter and golden syrup in a saucepan over a low heat and stir until just melted and smooth.

Remove from the heat and leave to cool until it begins to thicken enough to leave a trail when the spoon is lifted. Pour the icing over the top of the cake, allowing it to drizzle down the sides. Arrange the sweets over the top of the cake.

SERVES 10

175 g/6 oz soft margarine or spreadable butter, plus extra for greasing

175 g/6 oz caster sugar

3 eggs, beaten

175 g/6 oz plain flour

1 tsp baking powder

2 tbsp cocoa powder

55 g/2 oz white chocolate chips

40 g/1½ oz small coloured sweets, such as Smarties, to decorate

icing

175 g/6 oz milk chocolate or plain chocolate

100 g/3½ oz unsalted butter or margarine

1 tbsp golden syrup

VALENTINE CHOCOLATE HEART CAKE

SERVES 12

175 g/6 oz self-raising flour

2 tsp baking powder

55 g/2 oz cocoa powder

3 eggs

140 g/5 oz light muscovado sugar

150 ml/5 fl oz sunflower oil,
   plus extra for greasing

150 ml/5 fl oz single cream

fresh mint sprigs, to decorate

filling and topping

225 g/8 oz plain chocolate

250 ml/9 fl oz double cream

200 g/7 oz fresh or frozen
   raspberries

3 tbsp seedless raspberry jam

Preheat the oven to 180°C/350°F/Gas Mark 4. Grease a 20-cm/8-inch heart-shaped tin and line the base with baking paper.

Sift the flour, baking powder and cocoa powder into a large bowl. Beat the eggs with the sugar, oil and single cream. Make a well in the dry ingredients and add the egg mixture, then stir to mix thoroughly, beating to a smooth batter.

Pour the mixture into the prepared tin and bake in the preheated oven for 25–30 minutes, or until risen and firm to the touch. Leave to cool in the tin for 10 minutes, then turn out and finish cooling on a wire rack.

For the filling and topping, place the chocolate and double cream in a saucepan over a low heat and stir until melted. Remove from the heat and stir until the mixture cools slightly and begins to thicken.

Use a sharp knife to cut the cake in half horizontally. Spread the cut surface of each half with the raspberry jam, then top with about 3 tablespoons of the chocolate mixture. Scatter half the raspberries over the base and replace the top, pressing lightly.

Spread the remaining chocolate mixture over the top and sides of the cake, swirling with a palette knife. Top with the remaining raspberries and decorate with mint sprigs.

TRADITIONAL SIMNEL CAKE

Preheat the oven to 150°C/300°F/Gas Mark 2. Grease and line a 20-cm/8-inch round deep cake tin with baking paper.

Place the butter and sugar in a bowl and cream together with an electric whisk or wooden spoon until pale, light and fluffy. Gradually beat in the eggs, beating hard after each addition.

Sift together the flour, baking powder and mixed spice. Use a large metal spoon to fold into the creamed mixture. Stir in the lemon rind, currants, sultanas and mixed peel, mixing evenly. Spoon half the mixture into the prepared tin and smooth level.

Roll out 250 g/9 oz of the marzipan to a 20-cm/8-inch round and place over the mixture in the tin. Add the remaining cake mixture and smooth level.

Bake the cake in the preheated oven for 2¼–2¾ hours, or until firm and golden and the sides are beginning to shrink away from the tin. Leave to cool in the tin for 30 minutes, then turn out onto a wire rack to finish cooling.

Brush the top of the cake with apricot jam. Roll out two thirds of the remaining marzipan to a round to cover the top of the cake. Use a knife to mark a lattice design in the surface and pinch the edges to decorate.

Roll the remaining marzipan into 11 small balls and arrange around edge of the cake. Place under a hot grill for 30–40 seconds to brown lightly. Cool before storing.

SERVES 16

175 g/6 oz unsalted butter, plus extra for greasing

175 g/6 oz light muscovado sugar

3 eggs, beaten

225 g/8 oz plain flour

½ tsp baking powder

2 tsp ground mixed spice

finely grated rind of 1 small lemon

100 g/3½ oz currants

100 g/3½ oz sultanas

55 g/2 oz chopped mixed peel

700 g/1 lb 9 oz marzipan

3 tbsp apricot jam

EASTER CUPCAKES

Preheat the oven to 180°C/350°F/Gas Mark 4. Place 12 paper bun cases into a shallow bun tin.

Put the butter and sugar in a bowl and beat together until light and fluffy. Gradually add the eggs, beating well after each addition. Sift in the flour and cocoa powder and, using a large metal spoon, fold into the mixture. Spoon the mixture into the paper cases.

Bake in the preheated oven for 15–20 minutes, or until well risen and firm to the touch. Transfer to a wire rack and leave to cool.

To make the buttercream topping, put the butter in a bowl and beat until fluffy. Sift in the icing sugar and beat together until well mixed, adding the milk and vanilla extract.

When the cupcakes are cold, put the buttercream in a piping bag, fitted with a large star nozzle, and pipe a circle around the edge of each cupcake to form a nest. Place chocolate eggs in the centre of each nest to decorate.

MAKES 12

115 g/4 oz butter, softened, or soft margarine

115 g/4 oz caster sugar

2 eggs, lightly beaten

85 g/3 oz self-raising flour

25 g/1 oz cocoa powder

topping

85 g/3 oz butter, softened

175 g/6 oz icing sugar

1 tbsp milk

2–3 drops vanilla extract

250 g/9 oz mini sugar-coated chocolate eggs

ROSE-TOPPED WEDDING MUFFINS

MAKES 12

oil or melted butter, for greasing
(if using)

280 g/10 oz plain flour

1 tbsp baking powder

⅛ tsp salt

115 g/4 oz caster sugar

2 eggs

250 ml/9 fl oz milk

6 tbsp sunflower oil or 85 g/
3 oz butter, melted and cooled

1 tsp vanilla extract

12 ready-made sugar roses or
fresh rose petals or buds,
to decorate

icing

175 g/6 oz icing sugar

3–4 tsp hot water

Preheat the oven to 200°C/400°F/Gas Mark 6. Increase the quantity of ingredients according to the number of wedding guests invited, working in double quantities to make 24 muffins each time. Grease the appropriate number of muffin tins or line with paper muffin cases.

Sift together the flour, baking powder and salt into a large bowl. Stir in the caster sugar.

Lightly beat the eggs in a large jug or bowl, then beat in the milk, oil and vanilla extract. Make a well in the centre of the dry ingredients and pour in the beaten liquid ingredients. Stir gently until just combined; do not over-mix.

Spoon the mixture into the prepared muffin tin or tins. Bake in the preheated oven for about 20 minutes, until well risen, golden brown and firm to the touch.

Leave the muffins in the tin or tins for 5 minutes, then transfer to a wire rack and leave to cool. Store the muffins in the freezer until required.

On the day of serving, if using fresh flowers, rinse and leave to dry on kitchen paper. For the icing, sift the icing sugar into a bowl. Add the water and stir until the mixture is smooth and thick enough to coat the back of a wooden spoon. Spoon the icing on top of each muffin then top with a rose petal, rose bud or sugar rose.

HALLOWEEN SPIDER'S WEB CAKE

Preheat the oven to 170°C/325°F/Gas Mark 3. Grease an 18-cm/ 7-inch round cake tin and line the base with baking paper.

Cream together the butter and caster sugar until light and fluffy. Beat in the eggs and milk. Sift in the flour and baking powder, then fold in lightly and evenly using a metal spoon.

Spoon half the mixture into a separate bowl and stir in a few drops of orange food colouring, stirring to mix evenly. Place alternate spoonfuls of the plain and orange mixtures into the prepared cake tin, swirling lightly for a marbled effect. Bake in the preheated oven for 35–40 minutes, or until well-risen and firm to the touch. Leave to cool in the tin for 10 minutes, then turn out and finish cooling on a wire rack.

Reserve about 40 g/1½ oz of the icing and colour it with black food colouring, then colour the remaining icing with orange food colouring. Place the cake on a board or plate and brush the top and sides with apricot jam. Roll out the orange icing on a surface lightly dusted with icing sugar so it is large enough to cover the cake, then lift it onto the cake, smoothing with your hands. Trim the edges at the base, reserving the trimmings.

Place the icing sugar in a bowl and stir in enough water to mix to a paste, adding a few drops of black food colouring. Spoon into a small piping bag fitted with a medium plain nozzle, then pipe a spider's web design over the top of the cake. Shape about half of the black icing into an oval for the spider's body, then shape eight legs from the remaining black icing. Shape two eyes from the orange icing trimmings. Place on the web.

SERVES 8–10

115 g/4 oz unsalted butter, plus extra for greasing

115 g/4 oz caster sugar

2 eggs, beaten

3 tbsp milk

140 g/5 oz self-raising flour

½ tsp baking powder

a few drops of orange edible food colouring

topping

500 g/1 lb 2 oz ready-to-roll icing

a few drops black and orange edible food colourings

2 tbsp apricot jam, warmed

100 g/3½ oz icing sugar, plus extra for dusting

GOLDEN CHRISTMAS CAKE

Place the chopped apricots, mango and pineapple in a bowl with the sultanas, stem ginger and mixed peel. Stir in the orange rind, orange juice and brandy. Cover the bowl and leave to soak overnight.

Preheat the oven to 170°C/325°F/Gas Mark 3. Grease a 23-cm/9-inch round springform cake tin and line with baking paper.

Cream together the butter and sugar until the mixture is pale and fluffy. Add the eggs to the mixture, beating well between each addition. Stir in the honey.

Sift the flour with the allspice and fold into the mixture using a metal spoon. Add the soaked fruit and pecan nuts, stirring thoroughly to mix. Spoon the mixture into the prepared tin, spreading evenly, then make a slight dip in the centre.

Place the tin in the centre of the preheated oven and bake for 1½–2 hours, or until golden brown and firm to the touch and a skewer inserted into the centre comes out clean. Leave to cool in the tin.

Turn the cake out, remove the lining paper and re-wrap in clean baking paper and foil. Store in a cool place for at least 1 month before use. If desired, cover the cake with marzipan and ready-to-roll icing, following the pack instructions, and decorate with silver dragées.

SERVES 16–18

175 g/6 oz dried apricots, chopped

85 g/3 oz dried mango, chopped

85 g/3 oz dried pineapple, chopped

175 g/6 oz sultanas

55 g/2 oz chopped stem ginger

55 g/2 oz chopped mixed peel

finely grated rind and juice of 1 orange

4 tbsp brandy

175 g/6 oz unsalted butter, plus extra for greasing

100 g/3½ oz light muscovado sugar

4 eggs, beaten

2 tbsp clear honey

175 g/6 oz self-raising flour

2 tsp ground allspice

85 g/3 oz pecan nuts

topping (optional)

800 g/1 lb 12 oz marzipan

900 g/2 lb ready-to-roll icing

silver dragées

CHRISTMAS SNOWFLAKE MUFFINS

MAKES 12

oil or melted butter,
    for greasing (optional)

280 g/10 oz plain flour

1 tbsp baking powder

1 tsp allspice

⅛ tsp salt

115 g/4 oz soft dark brown sugar

2 eggs

100 ml/3½ fl oz milk

6 tbsp sunflower oil or 85 g/
    3 oz butter, melted and cooled

200 g/7 oz luxury mincemeat with
    cherries and nuts

450 g/1 lb ready-to-roll icing

icing sugar, for dusting

2½ tsp apricot jam

silver dragées, to decorate

Preheat the oven to 200°C/400°F/Gas Mark 6. Grease a 12-cup muffin tin or line with 12 paper muffin cases.

Sift together the flour, baking powder, allspice and salt into a large bowl. Stir in the brown sugar.

Lightly beat the eggs in a large jug or bowl then beat in the milk and oil. Make a well in the centre of the dry ingredients and pour in the beaten liquid ingredients and mincemeat. Stir gently until just combined; do not over-mix.

Spoon the mixture into the prepared muffin tin. Bake in the preheated oven for about 20 minutes, until well risen, golden brown and firm to the touch.

Leave the muffins in the tin for 5 minutes, then transfer to a wire rack and leave to cool.

Knead the icing until pliable. On a surface dusted with icing sugar, roll out the icing to a thickness of 5 mm/¼ inch. Using a 7-cm/2¾-inch fluted cutter, cut out 12 'snowflakes'.

Heat the apricot jam until runny, then brush over the tops of the muffins. Place a snowflake on top of each one, then decorate with silver dragées.

PANFORTE DI SIENA

Preheat the oven to 150°C/300°F/Gas Mark 2. Grease a 20-cm/ 8-inch round cake tin or loose-based tart tin and line the base with baking paper.

Toast the almonds under the grill until lightly browned, then place in a bowl. Toast the hazelnuts until the skins split. Place on a dry tea towel and rub off the skins. Coarsely chop the hazelnuts and add them to the almonds, together with the mixed peel.

Chop the apricots and pineapple fairly finely and add to the nuts, together with the orange rind. Mix well.

Sift the flour, cocoa and cinnamon into the nut mixture and mix well.

Put the sugar and honey into a saucepan and heat until the sugar dissolves. Boil gently for about 5 minutes, or until the mixture thickens and starts to turn a deeper shade of brown. Quickly add to the nut mixture and mix thoroughly. Spoon into the prepared tin and smooth the top using the back of a damp spoon.

Cook in the preheated oven for 1 hour. Remove the cake from the oven and leave in the tin until completely cool. Take out of the tin and carefully peel off the paper. Dust with a little icing sugar before serving.

SERVES 12

butter, for greasing

150 g/5½ oz whole almonds, split

115 g/4 oz hazelnuts

85 g/3 oz chopped mixed peel

55 g/2 oz dried apricots

55 g/2 oz glacé pineapple

grated rind of 1 large orange

70 g/2½ oz plain flour

2 tbsp cocoa powder

2 tsp ground cinnamon

115 g/4 oz caster sugar

175 g/6 oz clear honey

icing sugar, for dusting

STOLLEN

Put the currants, raisins, mixed peel and cherries in a bowl. Stir in the rum and set aside. Put the butter, milk and caster sugar in a saucepan and heat gently until the sugar has dissolved and the butter has just melted. Leave to cool slightly. Sift the flour, salt, nutmeg and cinnamon into a bowl. Crush the cardamom seeds and add them to the flour mixture. Stir in the yeast. Make a well in the centre and stir in the milk mixture, lemon rind and egg. Beat to form a soft dough.

Turn out the dough onto a floured work surface. With floured hands, knead the dough for about 5 minutes. It will be quite sticky, so add more flour if necessary. Knead the soaked fruit and flaked almonds into the dough until just combined. Place the dough in a clean, lightly oiled bowl. Cover with clingfilm and leave in a warm place for 1½ hours, or until doubled in size. Turn the dough onto a floured work surface and knead lightly for 1–2 minutes, then roll out to a 25-cm/10-inch square.

Roll the marzipan into a sausage shape slightly shorter than the length of the dough and place down the centre. Fold one side over to cover the marzipan. Repeat with the other side, overlapping in the centre. Seal the ends. Place the roll, seam-side down, on a greased baking sheet. Cover with oiled clingfilm and leave in a warm place until doubled in size. Preheat the oven to 190°C/375°F/Gas Mark 5. Bake the stollen for 40 minutes, or until it is golden and it sounds hollow when tapped underneath. Brush the hot stollen generously with melted butter and dredge heavily with icing sugar. Leave to cool on a wire rack.

SERVES 10

85 g/3 oz currants

55 g/2 oz raisins

35 g/1¼ oz chopped mixed peel

55 g/2 oz glacé cherries, rinsed, dried and quartered

2 tbsp dark rum

4 tbsp butter

175 ml/6 fl oz milk

3 tbsp golden caster sugar

375 g/13 oz strong white flour, plus extra for dusting

½ tsp salt

½ tsp ground nutmeg

½ tsp ground cinnamon

seeds from 3 cardamom pods

2 tsp easy-blend dried yeast

finely grated rind of 1 lemon

1 egg, beaten

40 g/1½ oz flaked almonds

oil, for greasing

175 g/6 oz marzipan

melted butter, for brushing

icing sugar, for dusting

SACHERTORTE

SERVES 10

175 g/6 oz plain chocolate, broken
  into pieces

140 g/5 oz unsalted butter,
  plus extra for greasing

140 g/5 oz caster sugar

6 eggs, separated

175 g/6 oz plain flour

icing

225 g/8 oz plain chocolate,
  broken into pieces

5 tbsp strong black coffee

175 g/6 oz icing sugar

6 tbsp apricot jam, warmed

Preheat the oven to 150°C/300°F/Gas Mark 2. Grease and line
a 23-cm/9-inch round springform cake tin.

Put the chocolate in a heatproof bowl set over a saucepan
of gently simmering water until melted. In a separate bowl,
beat the butter and 70 g/2½ oz of the sugar until pale and
fluffy. Add the egg yolks and beat well. Add the chocolate in
a thin stream, beating well. Sift in the flour and fold it into the
mixture. Whisk the egg whites until they stand in soft peaks.
Add the remaining sugar and whisk until glossy. Fold half the
egg white mixture into the chocolate mixture, then fold in
the remainder.

Spoon into the prepared tin and smooth the top. Bake in the
preheated oven for 1–1¼ hours, until a skewer inserted into
the centre comes out clean. Cool in the tin for 5 minutes, then
transfer to a wire rack to cool completely.

To make the icing, melt 175 g/6 oz of the chocolate and beat
in the coffee until smooth. Sift in the icing sugar and whisk
to give a thick icing. Halve the cake. Spread the jam over the
cut edges and sandwich together. Invert the cake on a wire
rack. Spoon the icing over the cake and spread to coat the top
and sides. Leave to set for 5 minutes, letting any excess drop
through the rack. Transfer to a serving plate and leave to set
for at least 2 hours.

To decorate, melt the remaining chocolate and spoon into
a small piping bag fitted with a fine plain nozzle. Pipe the
word 'Sacher' or 'Sachertorte' on top of the cake. Leave to set
before serving.

CHOCOLATE GANACHE CAKE

Preheat the oven to 180°C/350°F/Gas Mark 4. Lightly grease and line a 20-cm/8-inch round springform cake tin.

Beat the butter and sugar until light and fluffy. Gradually add the eggs, beating well after each addition. Sift the flour and cocoa powder together. Fold into the cake mixture. Fold in the melted chocolate.

Pour into the prepared tin and smooth the top. Bake in the preheated oven for 40 minutes, or until springy to the touch. Leave the cake to cool for 5 minutes in the tin, then turn out onto a wire rack and leave to cool completely. Cut the cake into two layers.

To make the ganache, place the cream in a saucepan and bring to the boil, stirring. Add the chocolate and stir until melted. Pour into a bowl, leave to cool, then chill for 2 hours, or until set and firm. Whisk the mixture until light and fluffy.

Reserve one third of the ganache. Use the remaining ganache to sandwich the cake together and spread over the top and sides.

Melt the cake covering and spread it over a large sheet of baking paper. Leave to cool until just set. Cut into strips a little wider than the height. Place the strips around the edge of the cake, overlapping them slightly.

Pipe the reserved ganache in tear drops or shells to cover the top of the cake. Leave to chill for 1 hour.

SERVES 10

175 g/6 oz butter, plus extra for greasing

175 g/6 oz caster sugar

4 eggs, lightly beaten

250 g/9 oz self-raising flour

1 tbsp cocoa powder

50 g/1¾ oz plain chocolate, melted

200 g/7 oz chocolate-flavoured cake covering

ganache

450 ml/16 fl oz double cream

375 g/13 oz plain chocolate, broken into pieces

RED VELVET CAKE

Preheat the oven to 190°C/375°F/Gas Mark 5. Grease two 23-cm/ 9-inch sandwich tins and line the bases with baking paper.

Place the butter, water and cocoa powder in a small saucepan and heat gently, without boiling, stirring until melted and smooth. Remove from the heat and leave to cool slightly.

Beat together the eggs, buttermilk, vanilla extract and food colouring until frothy. Beat in the butter mixture. Sift together the flour, cornflour and baking powder, then stir quickly and evenly into the mixture with the caster sugar.

Divide the mixture between the prepared tins and bake in the preheated oven for 25–30 minutes, or until risen and firm to the touch. Leave to cool in the tins for 3–4 minutes, then turn out and finish cooling on a wire rack.

For the frosting, beat together all the ingredients until smooth. Use about half of the frosting to sandwich the cakes together, then spread the remainder over the top, swirling with a palette knife.

(* If you prefer not to use synthetic food colouring, this can be replaced by 4 tablespoons of beetroot juice: you should reduce the water quantity to 2 tablespoons. If you have an electric juicer, 1 medium beetroot should yield about 4 tablespoons of juice.)

SERVES 12

225 g/8 oz unsalted butter, plus extra for greasing

4 tbsp water

55 g/2 oz cocoa powder

3 eggs

250 ml/9 fl oz buttermilk

2 tsp vanilla extract

2 tbsp red edible food colouring*

280 g/10 oz plain flour

55 g/2 oz cornflour

1½ tsp baking powder

280 g/10 oz caster sugar

frosting

250 g/9 oz full-fat soft cheese

40 g/1½ oz unsalted butter

3 tbsp caster sugar

1 tsp vanilla extract

HUMMINGBIRD CAKE

SERVES 10

250 g/9 oz plain flour

250 g/9 oz caster sugar

1 tsp ground cinnamon

1 tsp bicarbonate of soda

3 eggs, beaten

200 ml/7 fl oz sunflower oil, plus extra for greasing

100 g/3½ oz pecan nuts, roughly chopped, plus extra to decorate

3 ripe bananas (about 375 g/13 oz peeled weight), mashed

85 g/3 oz canned crushed pineapple (drained weight), plus 4 tbsp juice from the can

frosting

175 g/6 oz full-fat soft cheese

55 g/2 oz unsalted butter

1 tsp vanilla extract

400 g/14 oz icing sugar

Preheat the oven to 180°C/350°F/Gas Mark 4. Lightly grease three 23-cm/9-inch sandwich tins with oil and line the bases with baking paper.

Sift together the flour, caster sugar, cinnamon and bicarbonate of soda into a large bowl. Add the eggs, oil, pecan nuts, bananas pineapple and pineapple juice, and stir with a wooden spoon until evenly mixed.

Divide the mixture between the prepared tins, spreading evenly. Bake in the preheated oven for 25–30 minutes, or until golden brown and firm to the touch.

Remove the cakes from the oven and leave to cool for 10 minutes in the tins before turning out onto wire racks to cool.

For the frosting, beat together the soft cheese, butter and vanilla extract in a bowl until smooth. Sift in the icing sugar and mix until smooth.

Sandwich the cakes together with half of the frosting, spread the remaining frosting over the top, then sprinkle with pecan nuts to decorate.

WHITE CHOCOLATE COFFEE GATEAU

Preheat the oven to 180°C/350°F/Gas Mark 4. Grease two 20-cm/ 8-inch sandwich cake tins and line the bases with baking paper.

Place the butter and chocolate in a bowl set over a saucepan of hot, but not simmering, water and leave on a very low heat until just melted. Stir to mix lightly, then remove from the heat.

Place the caster sugar, eggs, coffee and vanilla extract in a large bowl set over a saucepan of hot water and whisk hard with an electric whisk until the mixture is pale and thick enough to leave a trail when the whisk is lifted.

Remove from the heat, sift in the flour and fold in lightly and evenly. Quickly fold in the butter and chocolate mixture, then divide the mixture between the prepared tins.

Bake in the preheated oven for 25–30 minutes, until risen, golden brown and springy to the touch. Leave to cool in the tins for 2 minutes, then run a knife around the edges to loosen and turn out onto a wire rack to cool.

For the frosting, place the chocolate and butter in a bowl set over a saucepan of hot water and heat gently until melted. Remove from the heat, stir in the crème fraîche, then add the icing sugar and coffee liqueur and mix until smooth. Chill the frosting for at least 30 minutes, stirring occasionally, until it becomes thick and glossy.

Use about one third of the frosting to sandwich the cakes together. Spread the remainder over the top and sides, swirling with a palette knife. Arrange the chocolate curls over the top of the cake and leave to set.

SERVES 8–10

40 g/1½ oz unsalted butter, plus extra for greasing

85 g/3 oz white chocolate

125 g/4½ oz caster sugar

4 large eggs, beaten

2 tbsp very strong black coffee

1 tsp vanilla extract

125 g/4½ oz plain flour

white chocolate curls, to decorate

frosting

175 g/6 oz white chocolate

85 g/3 oz unsalted butter

125 g/4½ oz crème fraîche

125 g/4½ oz icing sugar, sifted

1 tbsp coffee liqueur or very strong black coffee

CITRUS MOUSSE CAKE

Preheat the oven to 180°C/350°F/Gas Mark 4. Grease a 20-cm/ 8-inch round springform cake tin and and line the base with baking paper.

Beat the butter and sugar in a bowl until light and fluffy. Gradually add the eggs, beating well after each addition. Sift together the flour and cocoa and fold into the creamed mixture. Fold in the melted chocolate.

Pour into the prepared tin and level the top. Bake in the preheated oven for 40 minutes, or until springy to the touch. Leave to cool for 5 minutes in the tin, then turn out onto a wire rack and leave to cool completely. Cut the cold cake into two layers.

To make the orange mousse, beat the egg yolks and sugar until pale, then whisk in the orange juice. Sprinkle the gelatine over the water in a small bowl and allow to go spongy, then place over a saucepan of hot water and stir until dissolved. Stir into the egg yolk mixture.

Whip the cream until holding its shape, reserve a little for decoration and fold the rest into the mousse. Whisk the egg whites until standing in soft peaks, then fold in. Leave in a cool place until starting to set, stirring occasionally.

Place half of the cake in the tin. Pour in the mousse and press the second cake layer on top. Chill until set. Transfer to a serving plate, spoon teaspoonfuls of cream around the top and decorate the centre with orange segments.

SERVES 12

175 g/6 oz butter, plus extra for greasing

175 g/6 oz caster sugar

4 eggs, lightly beaten

200 g/7 oz self-raising flour

1 tbsp cocoa powder

50 g/1¾ oz orange-flavoured plain chocolate, melted

peeled orange segments, to decorate

mousse

2 eggs, separated

50 g/1¾ oz caster sugar

200 ml/7 fl oz freshly squeezed orange juice

2 tsp gelatine

3 tbsp water

300 ml/10 fl oz double cream

CHOCOLATE TRUFFLE TORTE

SERVES 10

butter, for greasing

55 g/2 oz caster sugar

2 eggs

25 g/1 oz plain flour

25 g/1 oz cocoa powder

4 tbsp strong black coffee

2 tbsp brandy

cocoa powder and icing sugar,
   to decorate

filling

600 ml/1 pint whipping cream

425 g/15 oz plain chocolate,
   broken into pieces

Preheat the oven to 220ºC/425ºF/Gas Mark 7. Grease and line a
23-cm/9-inch round springform cake tin.

Put the sugar and eggs in a heatproof bowl set over a saucepan of
gently simmering water. Whisk together until pale and resembling
the texture of mousse. Sift in the flour and cocoa and fold gently
into the mixture.

Pour into the prepared tin and bake in the preheated oven for
7–10 minutes, or until risen and firm to the touch. Transfer to a wire
rack to cool. Wash and dry the tin and return the cooled cake to the
tin. Mix together the coffee and brandy and brush over the cake.

To make the truffle filling, put the cream in a bowl and
whisk until just holding very soft peaks. Put the chocolate in a
heatproof bowl set over a saucepan of gently simmering water
until melted. Carefully fold the cooled melted chocolate into the
cream. Pour the chocolate mixture over the sponge. Chill until set.

To decorate the torte, sift cocoa powder over the top and
remove carefully from the tin. Using strips of card or baking
paper, sift bands of icing sugar over the torte to create a striped
pattern. To serve, cut into slices with a hot knife.

RASPBERRY VACHERIN

Preheat the oven to 140°C/275°F/Gas Mark 1. Draw three rectangles, measuring 10 x 25 cm/4 x 10 inches, on sheets of baking paper and place on two baking trays.

Whisk the egg whites in a mixing bowl until soft peaks form, then gradually whisk in half the sugar and continue whisking until the mixture is very stiff and glossy.

Carefully fold in the remaining sugar, the cornflour and the grated chocolate with a metal spoon or a palette knife.

Spoon the meringue mixture into a piping bag fitted with a 1-cm/½-inch plain nozzle and pipe lines across the rectangles.

Bake in the preheated oven for 1½ hours, changing the position of the baking trays halfway through. Without opening the oven door, turn off the oven and leave the meringues to cool inside the oven, then peel away the baking paper.

Place the chocolate in a heatproof bowl set over a saucepan of gently simmering water until melted. Spread the chocolate over two of the meringue layers. Leave to harden.

Place one chocolate-coated meringue on a plate and top with about one third of the cream and raspberries. Gently place the second chocolate-coated meringue on top and spread with half of the remaining cream and raspberries. Place the last meringue on the top and decorate with the remaining cream and raspberries.

Drizzle the melted chocolate over the top of the vacherin and serve.

SERVES 10

3 egg whites

175 g/6 oz caster sugar

1 tsp cornflour

25 g/1 oz plain chocolate, grated

filling & topping

175 g/6 oz plain chocolate, broken into pieces

450 ml/16 fl oz double cream, whipped

280 g/10 oz fresh raspberries

a little melted chocolate, to decorate

STRAWBERRY ROULADE

Preheat the oven to 220°C/425°F/Gas Mark 7. Line a 35 x 25-cm/ 14 x 10-inch Swiss roll tin with baking paper.

Place the eggs in a mixing bowl with the caster sugar. Place the bowl over a saucepan of hot, but not boiling, water and whisk until pale and thick.

Remove the bowl from the pan. Sift in the flour and fold into the egg mixture with the hot water. Pour the mixture into the prepared tin and bake in the preheated oven for about 8–10 minutes, until golden and springy to the touch.

Remove from the tin and transfer to a sheet of baking paper. Peel off the lining paper and roll up the sponge tightly along with the baking paper. Wrap in a clean tea towel and set aside to cool.

For the filling, mix together the fromage frais and almond extract. Cover and chill in the refrigerator until required. Wash, hull and slice the strawberries.

Unroll the sponge, spread the fromage frais mixture over it and sprinkle with the sliced strawberries. Roll the sponge up again (without the baking paper this time) and transfer to a serving plate. Sprinkle with the toasted flaked almonds and serve.

SERVES 8

3 large eggs

125 g/4½ oz caster sugar

125 g/4½ oz plain flour

1 tbsp hot water

1 tbsp toasted flaked almonds, to decorate

filling

200 ml/7 fl oz low-fat fromage frais

1 tsp almond extract

225 g/8 oz small strawberries

BLACK FOREST
ROULADE

SERVES 8–10

sunflower oil, for greasing

175 g/6 oz plain chocolate

2–3 tbsp kirsch or brandy

5 eggs

225 g/8 oz caster sugar

icing sugar, for dusting

filling

350 ml/12 fl oz double cream

1–2 tbsp kirsch or brandy

350 g/12 oz fresh black cherries, stoned, or 400 g/14 oz canned morello cherries, drained and stoned

Preheat the oven to 190°C/375°F/Gas Mark 5. Grease and line a 35 x 25-cm/14 x 10-inch Swiss roll tin.

Break the chocolate into small pieces and place in a heatproof bowl set over a saucepan of gently simmering water. Add the kirsch and heat gently, stirring until the mixture is smooth. Remove from the pan and set aside.

Place the eggs and caster sugar in a large heatproof bowl and set over the pan of gently simmering water. Whisk the eggs and sugar until very thick and creamy and the whisk leaves a trail when dragged across the surface. Remove the bowl from the heat and whisk in the cooled chocolate mixture.

Spoon into the prepared tin, then tap the tin lightly on the work surface to smooth the top. Bake in the preheated oven for 20 minutes, or until firm to the touch. Remove from the oven and immediately invert onto a sheet of baking paper that has been dusted with the icing sugar. Lift off the tin and lining paper, then roll up, encasing the baking paper in the roulade. Leave until cold.

For the filling, whip the cream until soft peaks form, then stir in the kirsch. Unroll the roulade and spread over the cream to within ¼ inch/5 mm of the edges. Scatter the cherries over the cream. Carefully roll up the roulade again and place on a serving platter.

BAKED LEMON CHEESECAKE

Preheat the oven to 180°C/350°F/Gas Mark 4. Lightly grease a 20-cm/8-inch round springform cake tin and line the base with non-stick baking paper.

Melt the butter and stir in the biscuit crumbs. Press into the base of the prepared cake tin. Chill until firm.

Meanwhile, finely grate the rind and squeeze the juice from the lemons. Add the ricotta, yogurt, eggs, cornflour and caster sugar, and whisk until a smooth batter is formed.

Carefully pour the mixture into the tin. Bake in the preheated oven for 40–45 minutes, or until just firm and golden brown.

Cool the cheesecake completely in the tin, then run a knife around the edge to loosen and turn out onto a serving plate. Decorate with lemon zest and dust with icing sugar.

SERVES 6–8

55 g/2 oz butter, plus extra
  for greasing

175 g/6 oz gingernut biscuits,
  crushed

3 lemons

300 g/10½ oz ricotta cheese

200 g/7 oz Greek-style yogurt

4 eggs

1 tbsp cornflour

100 g/3½ oz caster sugar

strips of lemon zest, to decorate

icing sugar, for dusting

BROWNIE BASE CHEESECAKE

Preheat the oven to 180°C/350°F/Gas Mark 4. Lightly grease and flour a 23-cm/9-inch square cake tin.

Melt the butter and chocolate in a saucepan over a low heat, stirring until smooth. Remove from the heat and beat in the sugar.

Add the eggs and milk, beating well. Stir in the flour, mixing just until blended. Spoon into the prepared tin, spreading evenly.

Bake in the preheated oven for 25 minutes. Remove from the oven and reduce the oven temperature to 160°C/325°F/Gas Mark 3.

For the topping, beat together the cheese, sugar, eggs and vanilla extract until well blended. Stir in the yogurt, then pour over the brownie base. Bake for a further 45–55 minutes, or until the centre is almost set.

Run a knife around the edge of the cheesecake to loosen from the tin. Leave to cool before removing from the tin. Chill in the refrigerator for 4 hours or overnight before cutting into slices. Drizzle with the melted chocolate and serve with chocolate-dipped strawberries.

SERVES 12

brownie base

115 g/4 oz unsalted butter, plus extra for greasing

115 g/4 oz plain chocolate

200 g/7 oz caster sugar

2 eggs, beaten

50 ml/2 fl oz milk

115 g/4 oz plain flour, plus extra for dusting

strawberries dipped in melted chocolate, to serve

topping

500 g/1 lb 2 oz soft cheese

125 g/4½ oz golden caster sugar

3 eggs, beaten

1 tsp vanilla extract

115 g/4 oz natural yogurt

melted chocolate, for drizzling

SMALL CAKES & BARS

LOW-FAT BLUEBERRY MUFFINS

Preheat the oven to 190°C/375°F/Gas Mark 5. Place 12 paper muffin cases in a muffin tin.

Sift the flour, bicarbonate of soda, salt and half the allspice into a large mixing bowl. Add 6 tablespoons of the sugar and mix together well.

In a separate bowl, whisk the egg whites together. Add the margarine, yogurt and vanilla extract and mix together well, then stir in the blueberries until thoroughly mixed. Add the fruit mixture to the dry ingredients, then gently stir until just combined. Do not overstir the mixture – it is fine for it to be a little lumpy.

Divide the mixture evenly between the paper cases (they should be about two-thirds full). Mix the remaining sugar with the remaining allspice, then sprinkle the mixture over the muffins.

Bake in the preheated oven for 25 minutes, or until risen and golden. Remove the muffins from the oven and serve warm, or place them on a wire rack to cool completely.

MAKES 12

225 g/8 oz plain flour

1 tsp bicarbonate of soda

¼ tsp salt

1 tsp allspice

115 g/4 oz caster sugar

3 large egg whites

3 tbsp low-fat margarine

150 ml/5 fl oz thick low-fat natural yogurt or blueberry-flavoured yogurt

1 tsp vanilla extract

85 g/3 oz fresh blueberries

LEMON & POPPY SEED MUFFINS

Preheat the oven to 190°C/375°F/Gas Mark 5. Place 12 paper muffin cases in a muffin tin.

Sift the flour and baking powder into a large bowl and stir in the sugar.

Heat a heavy-based frying pan over a medium–high heat and add the poppy seeds, then toast for about 30 seconds, shaking the pan to prevent them burning. Remove from the heat and add to the flour mixture.

Melt the butter, then beat with the egg, milk, lemon rind and lemon juice. Pour into the dry mixture and stir well to mix evenly to a soft, sticky dough. Add a little more milk if the mixture is too dry.

Spoon the mixture into the muffin cases, then bake in the preheated oven for 25–30 minutes, or until risen and golden brown. Place on a wire rack to cool.

MAKES 12

350 g/12 oz plain flour

1 tbsp baking powder

115 g/4 oz caster sugar

2 tbsp poppy seeds

55 g/2 oz unsalted butter

1 large egg, beaten

225 ml/8 fl oz milk

finely grated rind and juice of
   1 lemon

DOUBLE CHOCOLATE MUFFINS

MAKES 12

100 g/3½ oz butter, softened

125 g/4½ oz caster sugar

100 g/3½ oz dark muscovado sugar

2 eggs

150 ml/5 fl oz soured cream

5 tbsp milk

250 g/9 oz plain flour

1 tsp bicarbonate of soda

2 tbsp cocoa powder

190 g/6½ oz plain chocolate chips

Preheat the oven to 190°C/375°F/Gas Mark 5. Place 12 paper muffin cases in a muffin tin.

Put the butter, caster sugar and muscovado sugar into a bowl and beat well. Beat in the eggs, soured cream and milk until thoroughly mixed. Sift the flour, bicarbonate of soda and cocoa powder into a separate bowl and stir into the mixture. Add the chocolate chips and mix well.

Spoon the mixture into the paper cases. Bake in the preheated oven for 25–30 minutes. Remove from the oven and leave to cool for 10 minutes. Turn out onto a wire rack and leave to cool completely.

ICED FAIRY CAKES

Preheat the oven to 190°C/375°F/Gas Mark 5. Place 16 paper bun cases into a shallow bun tin.

Place the butter and caster sugar in a large bowl and cream together with a wooden spoon or electric mixer until pale and fluffy.

Gradually add the eggs, beating well after each addition. Fold in the flour lightly and evenly using a metal spoon.

Divide the mixture evenly between the bun cases and bake in the preheated oven for 15–20 minutes. Cool on a wire rack.

For the icing, sift the icing sugar into a bowl and stir in just enough of the water to mix to a smooth paste that is thick enough to coat the back of a wooden spoon. Stir in a few drops of food colouring, if using. Spread the icing over the fairy cakes and decorate as desired.

MAKES 16

115 g/4 oz unsalted butter, softened

115 g/4 oz caster sugar

2 eggs, beaten

115 g/4 oz self-raising flour

icing and decoration

200 g/7 oz icing sugar

about 2 tbsp warm water

a few drops of edible food colouring (optional)

sugar flowers, hundreds and thousands, glacé cherries, and/ or chocolate strands, to decorate

CHOCOLATE BUTTERFLY CAKES

Preheat the oven to 180°C/350°F/Gas Mark 4. Place 12 paper bun cases in a shallow bun tin.

Place the margarine, caster sugar, flour, eggs and cocoa powder in a large bowl, and beat with an electric whisk until the mixture is just smooth. Beat in the melted chocolate.

Spoon the mixture into the paper cases, filling them three-quarters full. Bake in the preheated oven for 15 minutes, or until springy to the touch. Transfer to a wire rack and leave to cool completely.

Meanwhile, make the lemon buttercream. Place the butter in a mixing bowl and beat until fluffy, then gradually beat in the icing sugar. Beat in the lemon rind and gradually add the lemon juice, beating well.

Cut the top off each cake, using a serrated knife. Cut each cake top in half. Spread or pipe the lemon buttercream over the cut surface of each cake and push the two cut pieces of cake top into the icing to form wings. Dust with icing sugar.

MAKES 12

125 g/4½ oz soft margarine

125 g/4½ oz caster sugar

150 g/5½ oz self-raising flour

2 large eggs

2 tbsp cocoa powder

25 g/1 oz plain chocolate, melted

icing sugar, for dusting

lemon buttercream

100 g/3½ oz unsalted butter, softened

225 g/8 oz icing sugar, sifted

grated rind of ½ lemon

1 tbsp lemon juice

HONEY & SPICE CAKES

MAKES 22–24

140 g/5 oz unsalted butter

100 g/3½ oz light muscovado
   sugar

100 g/3½ oz honey

200 g/7 oz self-raising flour

1 tsp ground allspice

2 eggs, beaten

22–24 whole blanched almonds

Preheat the oven to 180°C/350°F/Gas Mark 4. Place paper bun cases in two 12-cup shallow bun tins.

Place the butter, sugar and honey in a large saucepan and heat gently, stirring, until the butter is melted. Remove the pan from the heat.

Sift together the flour and allspice and stir into the mixture in the saucepan, then beat in the eggs, mixing to a smooth batter.

Spoon the mixture into the prepared tins and place an almond on top of each one. Bake in the preheated oven for 20–25 minutes, or until well risen and golden brown. Transfer to a wire rack to cool.

TOFFEE APPLE CAKES

Preheat the oven to 200°C/400°F/Gas Mark 6. Grease a 12-cup muffin tin (preferably non-stick).

Core and coarsely grate one of the apples. Slice the remaining apple into 5 mm/¼ inch thick wedges and toss in the lemon juice. Sift together the flour, baking powder and cinnamon, then stir in the sugar and grated apple.

Melt the butter and mix with the milk, apple juice and egg. Stir the liquid mixture into the dry ingredients, mixing lightly until just combined.

Spoon the mixture into the prepared muffin tin. Arrange two apple slices on top of each.

Bake in the preheated oven for 20–25 minutes or until risen, firm and golden brown. Run a knife round the edge of each bun to loosen, then turn out onto a wire rack to cool.

For the topping, place all the ingredients in a small saucepan and heat, stirring, until the sugar has dissolved. Increase the heat and boil rapidly for 2 minutes, or until slightly thickened and syrupy. Cool slightly, then drizzle over the cakes and leave to set.

MAKES 12

2 eating apples

1 tbsp lemon juice

250 g/9 oz plain flour

2 tsp baking powder

1½ tsp ground cinnamon

70 g/2½ oz light muscovado sugar

55 g/2 oz butter, plus extra
  for greasing

100 ml/3½ fl oz milk

100 ml/3½ fl oz apple juice

1 egg, beaten

topping

2 tbsp single cream

40 g/1½ oz light muscovado sugar

15 g/½ oz unsalted butter

MOLTEN-CENTRED CHOCOLATE CUPCAKES

Preheat the oven to 190°C/375°F/Gas Mark 5. Put eight paper bun cases into a bun tin.

Put the margarine, caster sugar, egg, flour and cocoa powder in a large bowl and, using an electric hand whisk, beat together until just smooth.

Spoon half of the mixture into the paper cases. Using a teaspoon, make an indentation in the centre of each cake. Break the chocolate evenly into eight squares and place a piece on top of each indentation, then spoon the remaining cake mixture on top.

Bake the cupcakes in the preheated oven for 20 minutes, or until well risen and springy to the touch. Leave the cupcakes to cool for 2–3 minutes before serving warm, dusted with sifted icing sugar.

SMALL CAKES & BARS

130

MAKES 8

55 g/2 oz soft margarine

55 g/2 oz caster sugar

1 large egg

85 g/3 oz self-raising flour

1 tbsp cocoa powder

55 g/2 oz plain chocolate

icing sugar, for dusting

DOUBLE CHOCOLATE BROWNIES

MAKES 9

115 g/4 oz butter, plus extra
    for greasing

115 g/4 oz plain chocolate, broken
    into pieces

300 g/10½ oz golden caster sugar

pinch of salt

1 tsp vanilla extract

2 large eggs

140 g/5 oz plain flour

2 tbsp cocoa powder

100 g/3½ oz white chocolate chips

fudge sauce

4 tbsp butter

225 g/8 oz golden caster sugar

150 ml/5 fl oz milk

250 ml/9 fl oz double cream

225 g/8 oz golden syrup

200 g/7 oz plain chocolate,
    broken into pieces

Preheat the oven to 180°C/350°F/Gas Mark 4. Grease an 18-cm/7-inch square cake tin and line the base with baking paper.

Place the butter and chocolate in a small heatproof bowl set over a saucepan of gently simmering water until melted. Stir until smooth. Leave to cool slightly. Stir in the sugar, salt and vanilla extract. Add the eggs, one at a time, and stir until blended.

Sift the flour and cocoa powder into the mixture and beat until smooth. Stir in the chocolate chips, then pour the mixture into the prepared tin. Bake in the preheated oven for 35–40 minutes, or until the top is evenly coloured and a cocktail stick inserted into the centre comes out almost clean. Leave to cool slightly while you prepare the sauce.

To make the fudge sauce, place the butter, sugar, milk, cream and golden syrup in a small saucepan and heat gently until the sugar has dissolved. Bring to the boil and stir for 10 minutes, or until the mixture is caramel-coloured. Remove from the heat and add the chocolate. Stir until smooth. Cut the brownies into squares and serve immediately with the sauce.

CAPPUCCINO BROWNIES

Preheat the oven to 180°C/350°F/Gas Mark 4. Grease a 28 x 18-cm/ 11 x 7-inch shallow cake tin and line the base with baking paper.

Sift the flour, baking powder and cocoa into a bowl and add the butter, caster sugar, eggs and coffee. Beat well, by hand or with an electric whisk, until smooth, then spoon into the prepared tin and smooth the top.

Bake in the preheated oven for 35–40 minutes, or until risen and firm. Leave to cool in the tin for 10 minutes, then turn out onto a wire rack and peel off the lining paper. Leave to cool completely.

To make the frosting, place the chocolate, butter and milk in a bowl set over a saucepan of gently simmering water and stir until the chocolate has melted. Remove the bowl from the pan and sift in the icing sugar. Beat until smooth, then spread over the cake. Dust the top of the cake with cocoa powder, then cut into squares.

MAKES 15

225 g/8 oz self-raising flour

1 tsp baking powder

1 tsp cocoa powder, plus extra for dusting

225 g/8 oz butter, softened, plus extra for greasing

225 g/8 oz golden caster sugar

4 eggs, beaten

3 tbsp instant coffee granules, dissolved in 2 tbsp hot water, cooled

white chocolate frosting

115 g/4 oz white chocolate, broken into pieces

55 g/2 oz butter, softened

3 tbsp milk

175 g/6 oz icing sugar

COCONUT BARS

Preheat the oven to 180°C/350°F/Gas Mark 4. Grease a 23-cm/ 9-inch square cake tin and line the base with non-stick baking paper.

Cream together the butter and caster sugar until pale and fluffy, then gradually beat in the eggs. Stir in the orange rind, orange juice and soured cream. Fold in the flour and desiccated coconut evenly using a metal spoon.

Spoon the mixture into the prepared cake tin and level the surface. Bake in the preheated oven for 35–40 minutes, or until risen and firm to the touch.

Leave to cool for 10 minutes in the tin, then turn out and finish cooling on a wire rack.

For the frosting, lightly beat the egg white, just enough to break it up, and stir in the icing sugar and desiccated coconut, adding enough orange juice to mix to a thick paste. Spread over the top of the cake, sprinkle with toasted shredded coconut, then leave to set before slicing into bars.

MAKES 10

125 g/4½ oz unsalted butter, plus extra for greasing

225 g/8 oz golden caster sugar

2 eggs, beaten

finely grated rind of 1 orange

3 tbsp orange juice

150 ml/5 fl oz soured cream

140 g/5 oz self-raising flour

85 g/3 oz desiccated coconut

toasted shredded coconut, to decorate

frosting

1 egg white

200 g/7 oz icing sugar

85 g/3 oz desiccated coconut

about 1 tbsp orange juice

BAKEWELL SLICES

MAKES 12

pastry
175 g/6 oz plain flour
125 g/4½ oz butter
25 g/1 oz caster sugar
1 egg yolk
about 1 tbsp cold water

filling
115 g/4 oz unsalted butter
115 g/4 oz caster sugar
115 g/4 oz ground almonds
3 eggs, beaten
½ tsp almond extract
4 tbsp raspberry jam
2 tbsp flaked almonds

For the pastry, sift the flour into a bowl and rub in the butter with your fingertips until the mixture resembles fine breadcrumbs. Stir in the sugar, then mix the egg yolk with the water and stir in to make a firm dough, adding a little more water if necessary. Wrap in clingfilm and chill in the refrigerator for about 15 minutes, until firm enough to roll out.

Preheat the oven to 200°C/400°F/Gas Mark 6. Roll out the dough and use to line a 23-cm/9-inch square tart tin or shallow cake tin. Prick the base and chill for 15 minutes.

Meanwhile, cream together the butter and sugar until pale and fluffy, then beat in the ground almonds, eggs and almond extract.

Spread the jam over the pastry base, then top with the almond mixture, spreading evenly. Sprinkle with the flaked almonds.

Bake in the preheated oven for 10 minutes, then reduce the heat to 180°C/350°F/Gas Mark 4 and bake for a further 25–30 minutes, or until the filling is golden brown and firm to the touch. Leave to cool in the tin, then cut into bars.

LEMON DRIZZLE BARS

Preheat the oven to 180°C/350°F/Gas Mark 4. Grease an 18-cm/7-inch square cake tin and line with non-stick baking paper.

Place the eggs, caster sugar and margarine in a mixing bowl and beat hard until smooth and fluffy. Stir in the lemon rind, then fold in the flour lightly and evenly. Stir in the milk, mixing evenly, then spoon into the prepared cake tin, smoothing level.

Bake in the preheated oven for 45–50 minutes, or until golden brown and firm to the touch. Remove from the oven and stand the tin on a wire rack.

To make the syrup, place the icing sugar and lemon juice in a small saucepan and heat gently, stirring until the sugar dissolves. Do not boil.

Prick the warm cake all over with a skewer, and spoon the hot syrup evenly over the top, allowing it to be absorbed.

Leave to cool completely in the tin, then turn out the cake, cut into 12 pieces and dust with a little icing sugar before serving.

MAKES 12

2 eggs

175 g/6 oz caster sugar

150 g/5½ oz soft margarine, plus extra for greasing

finely grated rind of 1 lemon

175 g/6 oz self-raising flour

125 ml/4 fl oz milk

icing sugar, for dusting

syrup

140 g/5 oz icing sugar

50 ml/2 fl oz fresh lemon juice

CINNAMON
SQUARES

Preheat the oven to 180°C/350°F/Gas Mark 4. Grease a 23-cm/
9-inch square cake tin and line the base with baking paper.

In a large mixing bowl, cream together the butter and caster
sugar until the mixture is light and fluffy.

Gradually add the eggs to the mixture, beating thoroughly after
each addition.

Sift the flour, bicarbonate of soda and cinnamon together
into the creamed mixture and fold in evenly using a metal spoon.

Spoon in the soured cream and sunflower seeds and mix gently
until well combined.

Spoon the mixture into the prepared tin and smooth the surface
with the back of a spoon or a knife. Bake in the preheated oven for
about 45 minutes, until the mixture is firm to the touch. Loosen the
edges with a round-bladed knife, then turn out onto a wire rack to
cool completely. Slice into squares before serving.

MAKES 16

225 g/8 oz butter, softened,
plus extra for greasing

225 g/8 oz caster sugar

3 eggs, lightly beaten

225 g/8 oz self-raising flour

½ tsp bicarbonate of soda

1 tbsp ground cinnamon

150 ml/5 fl oz soured cream

55 g/2 oz sunflower seeds

LAMINGTON CAKES

MAKES 16

5 eggs

150 g/5½ oz caster sugar

175 g/6 oz plain flour

55 g/2 oz unsalted butter, melted,
   plus extra for greasing

250 g/9 oz desiccated coconut

icing

500 g/1 lb 2 oz icing sugar

40 g/1½ oz cocoa powder

85 ml/3 fl oz boiling water

75 g/2¾ oz unsalted butter,
   melted

Preheat the oven to 180°C/350°F/Gas Mark 4. Grease a 20-cm/
8-inch square cake tin and line the base with baking paper.

Place the eggs and caster sugar in a large bowl set over a
saucepan of gently simmering water and whisk until pale and
thick enough to leave a trail when the whisk is lifted.

Remove from the heat, sift in the flour and fold in evenly. Fold
in the melted butter. Pour into the prepared tin and bake in the
preheated oven for 35–40 minutes, or until risen, golden and
springy to the touch.

Leave to cool in the tin for 2–3 minutes, then turn out onto
a wire rack to finish cooling. When cold, cut the cake into
16 squares.

For the icing, sift together the icing sugar and cocoa into a bowl
and stir in the water and butter, mixing until smooth. Spread out
the desiccated coconut on a large plate. Dip each piece of sponge
cake into the icing, using two palette knives to turn and coat
evenly. Place in the desiccated coconut and turn to coat evenly.
Put the cakes on a sheet of baking paper and leave to set.

NUTTY
FLAPJACKS

Preheat the oven to 180°C/350°F/Gas Mark 4. Grease a 23-cm/
9-inch square cake tin.

Place the rolled oats, hazelnuts and flour in a large mixing bowl
and stir together.

Place the butter, golden syrup and sugar in a saucepan over
a low heat and stir until melted. Pour onto the dry ingredients
and mix well. Spoon the mixture into the prepared cake tin and
smooth the surface with the back of a spoon.

Bake in the preheated oven for 20–25 minutes, or until golden
and firm to the touch. Mark into 16 pieces and leave to cool in
the tin. When completely cold, cut with a sharp knife and remove
from the tin.

MAKES 16

200 g/7 oz rolled oats

115 g/4 oz chopped hazelnuts

55 g/2 oz plain flour

115 g/4 oz butter, plus
extra for greasing

2 tbsp golden syrup

85 g/3 oz light muscovado sugar

CHOCOLATE PEANUT BUTTER SQUARES

Preheat the oven to 180°C/350°F/Gas Mark 4.

Finely chop the chocolate. Sift the flour and baking powder into a large bowl. Add the butter to the flour mixture and rub in using your fingertips until the mixture resembles breadcrumbs. Stir in the sugar, rolled oats and nuts.

Put a quarter of the mixture into a bowl and stir in the chopped chocolate. Set aside.

Stir the egg into the remaining mixture, then press into the base of a 30 x 20-cm/12 x 8-inch baking tin. Bake in the preheated oven for 15 minutes. Meanwhile, mix the condensed milk and peanut butter together. Pour the mixture over the base and spread evenly, then sprinkle the reserved chocolate mixture on top and press down lightly.

Return to the oven and bake for a further 20 minutes, until golden brown. Leave to cool in the tin, then cut into squares.

MAKES 20

300 g/10½ oz milk chocolate

350 g/12 oz plain flour

1 tsp baking powder

225 g/8 oz butter

350 g/12 oz soft light brown sugar

175 g/6 oz rolled oats

70 g/2½ oz chopped mixed nuts

1 egg, beaten

400 g/14 oz canned condensed milk

70 g/2½ oz crunchy peanut butter

CHOCOLATE CARAMEL SHORTBREAD

MAKES 12

115 g/4 oz butter, plus extra
    for greasing

175 g/6 oz plain flour

55 g/2 oz golden caster sugar

filling and topping

175 g/6 oz butter

115 g/4 oz golden caster sugar

3 tbsp golden syrup

400 g/14 oz canned condensed
    milk

200 g/7 oz plain chocolate,
    broken into pieces

Preheat the oven to 180°C/350°F/Gas Mark 4. Grease and line the base of a 23-cm/9-inch shallow square cake tin.

Place the butter, flour and sugar in a food processor and process until it begins to bind together. Press the mixture into the prepared tin and smooth the top. Bake in the preheated oven for 20–25 minutes, or until golden.

Meanwhile, make the filling. Place the butter, sugar, golden syrup and condensed milk in a saucepan and heat gently until the sugar has dissolved. Bring to the boil and simmer for 6–8 minutes, stirring constantly, until the mixture becomes very thick. Pour over the shortbread base and leave to chill in the refrigerator until firm.

To make the topping, melt the chocolate and leave to cool, then spread over the caramel. Chill in the refrigerator until set. Cut the shortbread into 12 pieces with a sharp knife and serve.

CHOCOLATE PEPPERMINT BARS

Preheat the oven to 180°C/350°F/Gas Mark 4. Grease and line a 30 x 20-cm/12 x 8-inch baking tin.

Beat the butter and sugar together until pale and fluffy. Stir in the flour until the mixture binds together.

Knead the mixture to form a smooth dough, then press into the prepared tin. Prick the surface all over with a fork. Bake in the preheated oven for 10–15 minutes, until lightly browned and just firm to the touch. Remove from the oven and leave to cool in the tin.

Sift the icing sugar into a bowl. Gradually add the water, then add the peppermint extract and food colouring, if using. Spread the icing over the base, then leave to set.

Melt the chocolate in a heatproof bowl set over a saucepan of gently simmering water, remove from the heat, then spread over the icing. Leave to set, then cut into slices.

MAKES 16

55 g/2 oz unsalted butter, plus extra for greasing

55 g/2 oz caster sugar

115 g/4 oz plain flour

175 g/6 oz icing sugar

1–2 tbsp warm water

½ tsp peppermint extract

2 tsp green edible food colouring (optional)

175 g/6 oz plain chocolate, broken into pieces

STRAWBERRY SHORTCAKES

Preheat the oven to 180°C/350°F/Gas Mark 4. Lightly grease a large baking tray.

Sift the flour, baking powder and caster sugar into a bowl. Rub in the butter with your fingertips until the mixture resembles breadcrumbs. Beat the egg with 2 tablespoons of the milk and stir into the dry ingredients with a fork to form a soft, but not sticky, dough, adding more milk if necessary.

Turn out the dough onto a lightly floured surface and roll out to a thickness of about 2 cm/¾ inch. Stamp out rounds using a 7-cm/2¾-inch biscuit cutter. Press the trimmings together lightly and stamp out more rounds.

Place the rounds on the prepared baking tray and brush the tops lightly with milk. Bake in the preheated oven for 12–15 minutes, until firm and golden brown. Place on a wire rack to cool.

For the filling, stir the vanilla extract into the mascarpone cheese with 2 tablespoons of the icing sugar. Reserve a few whole strawberries for decoration, then hull and slice the rest. Sprinkle with the remaining tablespoon of icing sugar.

Split the shortcakes in half horizontally. Spoon half the mascarpone mixture onto the bases and top with sliced strawberries. Spoon over the remaining mascarpone mixture and replace the shortcake tops. To serve, dust with icing sugar and top with the reserved whole strawberries.

SERVES 6

225 g/8 oz self-raising flour, plus extra for dusting

½ tsp baking powder

100 g/3½ oz golden caster sugar

85 g/3 oz unsalted butter, plus extra for greasing

1 egg, beaten

2–3 tbsp milk, plus extra for brushing

filling

1 tsp vanilla extract

250 g/9 oz mascarpone cheese

3 tbsp icing sugar, plus extra for dusting

400 g/14 oz strawberries

SCONES

MAKES 10–12

450 g/1 lb plain flour, plus extra
   for dusting

½ tsp salt

2 tsp baking powder

55 g/2 oz butter

2 tbsp caster sugar

250 ml/9 fl oz milk, plus extra
   for brushing

strawberry jam and clotted cream,
   to serve

Preheat the oven to 220°C/425°F/Gas Mark 7.

Sift the flour, salt and baking powder into a bowl. Rub in the butter using your fingertips until the mixture resembles breadcrumbs. Stir in the sugar. Make a well in the centre and pour in the milk. Stir in using a palette knife and bring together to make a soft dough.

Turn the mixture onto a floured surface and lightly flatten the dough until it is of an even thickness, about 1 cm/½ inch. Don't be heavy-handed; scones need a light touch.

Cut out the scones using a 6-cm/2½-inch biscuit cutter and place on a baking tray.

Brush with a little milk and bake in the preheated oven for 10–12 minutes, until golden and well risen. Cool on a wire rack and serve freshly baked with strawberry jam and clotted cream.

ROCK
CAKES

Preheat the oven to 200°C/400°F/Gas Mark 6. Lightly grease two baking trays.

Sift the flour and baking powder into a large bowl and rub in the butter using your fingertips. Stir in the muscovado sugar, mixed dried fruit and lemon rind.

Beat the egg lightly with a tablespoon of the milk and stir into the flour mixture, adding a little more milk if necessary, until it starts to bind together to form a moist but firm dough.

Spoon small heaps of the mixture onto the prepared baking trays. Sprinkle with the demerara sugar.

Bake in the preheated oven for 15–20 minutes, or until golden brown and firm. Use a palette knife to transfer the cakes onto a wire rack to cool.

MAKES 8–10

225 g/8 oz plain flour

2 tsp baking powder

115 g/4 oz unsalted butter, plus extra for greasing

85 g/3 oz light muscovado sugar

85 g/3 oz mixed dried fruit

finely grated rind of 1 lemon

1 egg

1–2 tbsp milk

2 tsp demerara sugar

CHOCOLATE MERINGUES

Preheat the oven to 140°C/275°F/Gas Mark 1. Line two baking trays with baking paper.

Whisk the egg whites until soft peaks form, then gradually whisk in half the caster sugar. Continue whisking until the mixture is very stiff and glossy.

Carefully fold in the remaining sugar, cornflour and grated chocolate with a metal spoon or palette knife.

Spoon the mixture into a piping bag fitted with a large star or plain nozzle. Pipe 16 large rosettes or mounds onto the prepared baking trays.

Bake in the preheated oven for about 1 hour, changing the position of the baking trays after 30 minutes. Without opening the oven door, turn off the oven and leave the meringues to cool in the oven. Once cold, carefully peel off the baking paper.

Melt the plain chocolate in a heatproof bowl set over a saucepan of gently simmering water and carefully spread it over the bases of the meringues. Stand them upside down on a wire rack until the chocolate has set. Whip the cream, icing sugar and brandy, if using, until the cream holds its shape, then use to sandwich the chocolate-coated meringues together in pairs.

MAKES 8

4 egg whites

200 g/7 oz caster sugar

1 tsp cornflour

40 g/1½ oz plain chocolate, grated

filling

100 g/3½ oz plain chocolate

150 ml/5 fl oz double cream

1 tbsp icing sugar

1 tbsp brandy (optional)

ALMOND MACAROONS

1 egg white

85 g/3 oz ground almonds

85 g/3 oz caster sugar, plus extra
   for rolling

1/2 tsp almond extract

6–7 blanched almonds, split in half

Preheat the oven to 180°C/350°F/Gas Mark 4. Line two baking
trays with baking paper.

   Beat the egg white with a fork until frothy, then stir in the
ground almonds, sugar and almond extract, mixing to form a
sticky dough.

   Using lightly sugared hands, roll the dough into small balls and
place on the prepared baking trays. Press an almond half into the
centre of each.

   Bake in the preheated oven for 15–20 minutes, or until pale
golden. Place on a wire rack to cool.

SMALL CAKES & BARS

163

MADELEINES

SMALL CAKES & BARS

Preheat the oven to 190°C/375°F/Gas Mark 5. Lightly grease 30 holes in two to three standard-sized madeleine tins.

Place the eggs, egg yolk, vanilla extract and sugar in a large bowl and whisk with an electric hand mixer until very pale and thick.

Sift in the flour and baking powder and fold in lightly and evenly using a metal spoon. Fold in the melted butter evenly.

Spoon the mixture into the prepared tins, filling to about three-quarters full. Bake in the preheated oven for 8–10 minutes, until risen and golden.

Remove the cakes carefully from the tins and cool on a wire rack. They are best served the day they are made.

MAKES 30

3 eggs

1 egg yolk

1 tsp vanilla extract

140 g/5 oz caster sugar

140 g/5 oz plain flour

1 tsp baking powder

140 g/5 oz unsalted butter, melted and cooled, plus extra for greasing

PIES & PASTRIES

APPLE PIE

To make the pastry, sift the flour and salt into a mixing bowl. Add the butter and lard, and rub in with your fingertips until the mixture resembles fine breadcrumbs. Add enough cold water to mix to a firm dough. Wrap in clingfilm and chill in the refrigerator for 30 minutes.

Preheat the oven to 220°C/425°F/Gas Mark 7. Roll out almost two thirds of the pastry thinly and use to line a deep 23-cm/ 9-inch pie plate.

For the filling, mix the apples with the sugar and spices, and pack into the pastry case – the filling can come up above the rim. Add the water, if needed, particularly if the apples are not very juicy.

Roll out the remaining pastry to form a lid. Dampen the edges of the pie rim with water and position the lid, pressing the edges firmly together. Trim and crimp the edges.

Use the pastry trimmings to cut out leaves or other shapes to decorate the top of the pie. Dampen and attach. Glaze the top of the pie with beaten egg or milk, make one or two slits in the top and place the pie on a baking tray.

Bake in the preheated oven for 20 minutes, then reduce the temperature to 180°C/350°F/Gas Mark 4 and bake for a further 30 minutes, or until the pastry is a light golden brown. Serve hot or cold, sprinkled with sugar.

SERVES 6–8

pastry

175 g/6 oz plain flour

pinch of salt

85 g/3 oz butter or margarine, cut into small pieces

85 g/3 oz lard or white vegetable fat, cut into small pieces

about 1–2 tbsp water

beaten egg or milk, for glazing

filling

750 g–1 kg/1 lb 10 oz–2 lb 4 oz cooking apples, peeled, cored and sliced

125 g/4½ oz soft light brown or caster sugar, plus extra for sprinkling

½–1 tsp ground cinnamon, mixed spice or ground ginger

about 1–2 tbsp water

LATTICED CHERRY PIE

To make the pastry, sift the flour and baking powder into a large bowl. Stir in the mixed spice, salt and sugar. Rub in the butter with your fingertips until the mixture resembles fine breadcrumbs. Add the beaten egg and mix to a firm dough. Cut the dough in half and roll each half into a ball. Wrap in clingfilm and chill in the refrigerator for 30 minutes.

Preheat the oven to 220°C/425°F/Gas Mark 7. Grease a 23-cm/9-inch round tart tin. Roll out the pastry into two 30-cm/12-inch rounds and use one to line the tart tin.

To make the filling, put half the cherries and the sugar into a large saucepan. Bring to a simmer over a low heat, stirring, for 5 minutes, or until the sugar has melted. Stir in the almond extract, brandy and mixed spice. In a separate bowl, mix the cornflour and water to form a paste. Remove the saucepan from the heat, stir in the cornflour paste, then return to the heat and stir constantly until the mixture boils and thickens. Leave to cool a little. Stir in the remaining cherries, pour into the pastry case, then dot with the butter.

Cut the remaining pastry round into long strips about 1 cm/½ inch wide. Lay five strips evenly across the top of the filling in the same direction. Now lay six strips crossways over the strips, folding under every other strip to form a lattice. Trim off the edges and seal with water. Use your fingers to crimp around the rim, then brush the top with beaten egg. Cover with foil, then bake in the preheated oven for 30 minutes. Discard the foil, then bake for a further 15 minutes, or until golden.

SERVES 8

pastry

140 g/5 oz plain flour, plus extra for dusting

¼ tsp baking powder

½ tsp mixed spice

½ tsp salt

50 g/1¾ oz caster sugar

55 g/2 oz cold unsalted butter, diced, plus extra for greasing

1 egg, beaten, plus extra for glazing

filling

900 g/2 lb stoned fresh cherries, or canned cherries, drained

150 g/5 oz caster sugar

½ tsp almond extract

2 tsp cherry brandy

¼ tsp mixed spice

2 tbsp cornflour

2 tbsp water

25 g/1 oz butter

ONE ROLL FRUIT PIE

SERVES 8

175 g/6 oz plain flour, plus extra
   for dusting

100 g/3½ oz butter, diced, plus
   extra for greasing

1 tbsp water

1 egg, separated

crushed sugar cubes,
   for sprinkling

filling

600 g/1 lb 5 oz prepared fruit,
   such as rhubarb, gooseberries
   or plums

85 g/3 oz soft light brown sugar

1 tbsp ground ginger

Place the flour in a large bowl, add the butter and rub in with your fingertips until the mixture resembles breadcrumbs. Add the water and mix together to form a soft dough. Cover and leave to chill in the refrigerator for 30 minutes.

Preheat the oven to 200°C/400°F/Gas Mark 6. Grease a large baking tray. Roll out the dough on a lightly floured work surface, to a round 35 cm/14 inches in diameter. Transfer the round to the centre of the prepared baking tray and brush with the egg yolk.

To make the filling, mix the fruit with the sugar and ground ginger and pile it into the centre of the pastry. Turn in the edges of the pastry all the way around. Brush the surface of the pastry with the egg white and sprinkle with the crushed sugar cubes.

Bake in the preheated oven for 35 minutes, or until golden brown. Transfer to a serving plate and serve warm.

TARTE TATIN

Preheat the oven to 220°C/425°F/Gas Mark 7.

For the pastry, sift the flour into a bowl. Rub in the butter with your fingertips until the mixture resembles fine breadcrumbs. Stir in the sugar, then add the egg yolks and water, mixing lightly until it just binds together. Wrap in clingfilm and chill in the refrigerator for 10–15 minutes.

Meanwhile, for the filling, place the butter and sugar in a heavy-based saucepan with the water. Heat gently until the butter has melted, then bring to the boil. Boil rapidly, stirring occasionally, until the mixture turns to a rich, golden caramel colour. Pour quickly into a 23-cm/9-inch round cake tin (this needs to be 5 cm/2 inches deep with a rigid base), tilting to cover the base.

Peel, core and thickly slice the apples, toss with the lemon juice and arrange over the caramel in the tin.

Roll out the pastry on a lightly floured surface to a round large enough to fit the tin. Lift the pastry onto the apples and tuck in the edges.

Place on a baking tray and bake in the preheated oven for about 40 minutes, or until the pastry is golden. Allow to stand for 10 minutes, then carefully invert onto a serving plate.

SERVES 6

pastry

175 g/6 oz plain flour, plus extra for dusting

100 g/3½ oz cold unsalted butter

3 tbsp caster sugar

2 egg yolks

2–3 tbsp water

filling

85 g/3 oz unsalted butter

140 g/5 oz caster sugar

1 tbsp water

6–7 eating apples

2 tbsp lemon juice

PLUM CRUMBLE TART

Preheat the oven to 180°C/350°F/Gas Mark 4 and preheat a baking tray.

Sift the flour, cornflour and baking powder into a large bowl and rub in the butter with your fingertips. Stir in the nuts and sugar with just enough milk to bind together.

Remove about a quarter of the mixture, cover and place in the refrigerator. Gently knead together the remaining mixture and press into the base and sides of a 20-cm/8-inch loose-based round tart tin.

For the filling, halve, stone then quarter the plums and toss with the cornflour, sugar and orange rind. Arrange the plums over the pastry.

Remove the reserved dough from the refrigerator and, using your fingertips, crumble over the plums.

Place the tart on the baking tray and bake in the preheated oven for 40–45 minutes, until lightly browned and bubbling. Serve cut into slices with crème fraîche.

SERVES 8–10

dough
175 g/6 oz plain flour

1 tbsp cornflour

½ tsp baking powder

100 g/3½ oz unsalted butter

40 g/1½ oz hazelnuts, finely chopped

40 g/1½ oz caster sugar

2–3 tbsp milk

filling
400 g/14 oz ripe red plums

1 tbsp cornflour

3 tbsp caster sugar

finely grated rind of 1 small orange

crème fraîche or Greek-style yogurt, to serve

PEAR TART WITH CHOCOLATE SAUCE

SERVES 6

100 g/3½ oz plain flour

25 g/1 oz ground almonds

60 g/2¼ oz block margarine, plus extra for greasing

about 3 tbsp water

filling

50 g/1¾ oz butter

50 g/1¾ oz caster sugar

2 eggs, beaten

100 g/3½ oz ground almonds

2 tbsp cocoa powder

a few drops of almond extract

400 g/14 oz canned pear halves in natural juice, drained

chocolate sauce

4 tbsp caster sugar

3 tbsp golden syrup

100 ml/3½ fl oz water

175 g/6 oz plain chocolate, broken into pieces

25 g/1 oz butter

Preheat the oven to 200°C/400°F/Gas Mark 6. Lightly grease a 20-cm/8-inch round tart tin.

Sift the flour into a mixing bowl and stir in the ground almonds. Rub in the margarine with your fingertips until the mixture resembles breadcrumbs. Add enough water to mix to a soft dough. Cover, chill in the freezer for 10 minutes, then roll out and use to line the prepared tin. Prick the base with a fork and chill again.

To make the filling, beat the butter and sugar until light and fluffy. Beat in the eggs, then fold in the ground almonds, cocoa powder and almond extract. Spread the chocolate mixture in the pastry case. Thinly slice each pear widthways, flatten slightly, then arrange the pears on top of the chocolate mixture, pressing down lightly. Bake in the preheated oven for 30 minutes, or until the filling has risen. Cool slightly and transfer to a serving plate, if wished.

To make the chocolate sauce, place the sugar, golden syrup and water in a saucepan and heat gently, stirring until the sugar dissolves. Boil gently for 1 minute. Remove from the heat, add the chocolate and butter and stir until melted and well combined. Serve with the tart.

LEMON
MERINGUE PIE

To make the pastry, sift the flour into a bowl. Rub in the butter with your fingertips until the mixture resembles fine breadcrumbs. Mix in the remaining ingredients. Knead briefly on a lightly floured work surface. Wrap in clingfilm and chill in the refrigerator for 30 minutes.

Preheat the oven to 180°C/350°F/Gas Mark 4. Grease a 20-cm/ 8-inch round tart tin. Roll out the pastry to a thickness of 5 mm/ ¼ inch, then use it to line the base and sides of the tin. Prick all over with a fork, line with baking paper and fill with baking beans. Bake in the preheated oven for 15 minutes. Remove the pastry case from the oven and take out the paper and beans. Reduce the temperature to 150°C/300°F/Gas Mark 2.

For the filling, mix the cornflour with a little of the water to form a paste. Put the remaining water in a saucepan. Stir in the lemon juice and rind and cornflour paste. Bring to the boil, stirring. Cook for 2 minutes. Cool a little. Stir in five tablespoons of the caster sugar and the egg yolks, and pour into the pastry case.

Whisk the egg whites in a clean, grease-free bowl until stiff. Gradually whisk in the remaining caster sugar and spread over the pie. Bake for a further 40 minutes. Remove from the oven, cool and serve.

SERVES 6–8

pastry

150 g/5½ oz plain flour, plus extra for dusting

85 g/3 oz butter, cut into small pieces, plus extra for greasing

35 g/1¼ oz icing sugar, sifted

finely grated rind of ½ lemon

½ egg yolk, beaten

1½ tbsp milk

filling

3 tbsp cornflour

300 ml/10 fl oz water

juice and grated rind of 2 lemons

175 g/6 oz caster sugar

2 eggs, separated

KEY LIME PIE

Preheat the oven to 160°C/325°F/Gas Mark 3. Lightly grease a 23-cm/9-inch round tart tin, about 4 cm/1½ inches deep.

To make the crumb crust, put the biscuits, sugar and cinnamon in a food processor and process until fine crumbs form – do not overprocess to a powder. Add the melted butter and process again until moistened.

Tip the crumb mixture into the prepared tart tin and press over the base and up the side. Place the tart tin on a baking tray and bake in the preheated oven for 5 minutes.

Meanwhile, beat the condensed milk, lime juice, lime rind and egg yolks together in a bowl until well blended.

Remove the tart tin from the oven, pour the filling into the crumb crust and spread out to the edges. Return to the oven for a further 15 minutes, or until the filling is set around the edges but still wobbly in the centre.

Leave to cool completely on a wire rack, then cover and chill for at least 2 hours. Serve spread thickly with whipped cream.

SERVES 8

crumb crust

175 g/6 oz digestive or ginger biscuits

2 tbsp caster sugar

½ tsp ground cinnamon

70 g/2½ oz butter, melted, plus extra for greasing

filling

400 ml/14 fl oz canned condensed milk

125 ml/4 fl oz freshly squeezed lime juice

finely grated rind of 3 limes

4 egg yolks

whipped cream, to serve

SWEET PUMPKIN PIE

SERVES 6

.8 kg/4 lb sweet pumpkin, halved and deseeded, stem and stringy bits removed

40 g/5 oz plain flour, plus extra for dusting

¼ tsp baking powder

1½ tsp ground cinnamon

¾ tsp ground nutmeg

¾ tsp ground cloves

1 tsp salt

50 g/1¾ oz caster sugar

55 g/2 oz cold unsalted butter, diced, plus extra for greasing

3 eggs

400 ml/14 fl oz canned condensed milk

½ tsp vanilla extract

1 tbsp demerara sugar

streusel topping

2 tbsp plain flour

4 tbsp demerara sugar

1 tsp ground cinnamon

2 tbsp cold unsalted butter, diced

75 g/2¾ oz pecan nuts, chopped

75 g/2¾ oz walnuts, chopped

Preheat the oven to 190°C/375°F/Gas Mark 5. Put the pumpkin halves, face down, in a shallow baking tin and cover with foil. Bake in the preheated oven for 1½ hours, then leave to cool. Scoop out the flesh and purée in a food processor. Drain off any excess liquid. Cover and chill.

Grease a 23-cm/9-inch round tart tin. To make the pastry, sift the flour and baking powder into a large bowl. Stir in ½ teaspoon of the cinnamon, ¼ teaspoon of the nutmeg, ¼ teaspoon of the cloves, ½ teaspoon of the salt and all the caster sugar. Rub in the butter with your fingertips until the mixture resembles fine breadcrumbs, then make a well in the centre. Lightly beat one of the eggs and pour it into the well. Mix together with a wooden spoon, then shape the dough into a ball. Place the dough on a lightly floured surface, roll out and use to line the prepared tin. Trim the edges, then cover and chill for 30 minutes.

Preheat the oven to 220°C/425°F/Gas Mark 7. Put the pumpkin purée in a large bowl, then stir in the condensed milk and the remaining eggs. Add the remaining spices and salt, then stir in the vanilla extract and demerara sugar. Pour into the pastry case and bake in the preheated oven for 15 minutes.

Meanwhile, make the topping. Mix the flour, demerara sugar and cinnamon in a bowl, rub in the butter, then stir in the nuts. Remove the pie from the oven and reduce the heat to 180°C/350°F/Gas Mark 4. Sprinkle over the topping, then bake for a further 35 minutes.

SWEET POTATO PIE

To make the pastry, sift the flour, salt and caster sugar into a bowl. Add the butter and white vegetable fat to the bowl and rub in with your fingertips until the mixture resembles fine breadcrumbs. Sprinkle over 2 tablespoons of the water and mix with a fork to make a soft dough. If the pastry is too dry, sprinkle in the extra ½ tablespoon of water. Wrap the dough in clingfilm and chill in the refrigerator for at least 1 hour.

Meanwhile, bring a large saucepan of water to the boil over a high heat. Add the sweet potatoes and cook for 15 minutes. Drain, then cool under cold running water. When cool, cut each into eight wedges. Place the potatoes in a bowl and beat in the eggs and brown sugar until very smooth. Beat in the remaining ingredients, then set aside until required.

Preheat the oven to 220°C/425°F/Gas Mark 7. Roll out the pastry on a lightly floured work surface into a thin 28-cm/ 11-inch round and use to line a 23-cm/9-inch round tart tin, about 4 cm/1½ inches deep. Trim off the excess pastry and press a floured fork around the edge. Prick the base of the pastry case all over with the fork. Line with baking paper and fill with baking beans. Bake in the preheated oven for 12 minutes, until lightly golden. Remove from the oven and take out the paper and beans.

Pour the filling into the pastry case and return to the oven for a further 10 minutes. Reduce the oven temperature to 160°C/325°F/Gas Mark 3 and bake for a further 35 minutes, or until a knife inserted into the centre comes out clean. Leave to cool on a wire rack. Serve warm or at room temperature.

SERVES 8

pastry

175 g/6 oz plain flour, plus extra for dusting

½ tsp salt

¼ tsp caster sugar

50 g/1¾ oz butter, diced

40 g/1½ oz white vegetable fat, diced

1–2½ tbsp cold water

filling

500 g/1 lb 2 oz orange-fleshed sweet potatoes, peeled

3 eggs, beaten

100 g/3½ oz soft light brown sugar

350 ml/12 fl oz canned condensed milk

40 g/1½ oz butter, melted

2 tsp vanilla extract

1 tsp ground cinnamon

1 tsp ground nutmeg

½ tsp salt

PECAN PIE

For the pastry, place the flour in a bowl and rub in the butter with your fingertips until it resembles fine breadcrumbs. Stir in the caster sugar and add enough cold water to mix to a firm dough. Wrap in clingfilm and chill for 15 minutes, until firm enough to roll out.

Preheat the oven to 200°C/400°F/Gas Mark 6. Roll out the pastry on a lightly floured surface and use to line a 23-cm/9-inch loose-based round tart tin. Prick the base with a fork. Chill for 15 minutes.

Place the tart tin on a baking tray and line with a sheet of baking paper and baking beans. Bake blind in the preheated oven for 10 minutes. Remove the baking beans and paper and bake for a further 5 minutes. Reduce the oven temperature to 180°C/350°F/Gas Mark 4.

For the filling, place the butter, muscovado sugar and golden syrup in a saucepan and heat gently until melted. Remove from the heat and quickly beat in the eggs and vanilla extract.

Roughly chop the pecans and stir into the mixture. Pour into the pastry case and bake for 35–40 minutes, until the filling is just set. Serve warm or cold.

SERVES 8

pastry

200 g/7 oz plain flour, plus extra for dusting

115 g/4 oz unsalted butter

2 tbsp caster sugar

a little cold water

filling

70 g/2½ oz unsalted butter

100 g/3½ oz light muscovado sugar

140 g/5 oz golden syrup

2 large eggs, beaten

1 tsp vanilla extract

115 g/4 oz pecan nuts

MISSISSIPPI MUD PIE

SERVES 8

pastry

225 g/8 oz plain flour, plus extra for dusting

2 tbsp cocoa powder

140 g/5 oz butter

2 tbsp caster sugar

1–2 tbsp cold water

filling

175 g/6 oz butter

350 g/12 oz soft dark brown sugar

4 eggs, lightly beaten

4 tbsp cocoa powder, sifted

150 g/5½ oz plain chocolate, broken into pieces

300 ml/10 fl oz single cream

1 tsp chocolate extract

to decorate

425 ml/15 fl oz double cream, whipped

chocolate flakes and curls

To make the pastry, sift the flour and cocoa powder into a mixing bowl. Rub in the butter with your fingertips until the mixture resembles fine breadcrumbs. Stir in the sugar and enough cold water to mix to a soft dough. Wrap the dough in clingfilm and chill in the refrigerator for 15 minutes.

Preheat the oven to 190°C/375°F/Gas Mark 5. Roll out the pastry on a lightly floured work surface and use to line a 23-cm/9-inch loose-based round tart tin. Line with baking paper and fill with baking beans. Bake in the preheated oven for 15 minutes. Remove the paper and beans from the pastry case and cook for a further 10 minutes, until crisp.

To make the filling, beat the butter and sugar together in a bowl and gradually beat in the eggs with the cocoa powder. Place the chocolate in a heatproof bowl set over a saucepan of gently simmering water until melted. Beat the melted chocolate into the butter mixture with the single cream and chocolate extract.

Reduce the oven temperature to 160°C/325°F/Gas Mark 3. Pour the mixture into the pastry case and bake for 45 minutes, or until the filling has set gently.

Leave to cool completely, then transfer the pie to a serving plate. Cover with the whipped cream and decorate with chocolate flakes and curls, then chill until ready to serve.

STRAWBERRY TARTLETS

To make the pastry, sift the flour and icing sugar into a bowl. Chop the butter into small pieces and add to the flour with the egg yolk, mixing with your fingertips and adding a little water, if necessary, to mix to a soft dough. Cover and place in the refrigerator to rest for 15 minutes.

Preheat the oven to 200°C/400°F/Gas Mark 6. Roll out the pastry and use to line four 9-cm/3½-inch tartlet tins. Prick the bases with a fork, line with baking paper and fill with baking beans, then bake blind in the preheated oven for 10 minutes. Remove the paper and beans and bake for a further 5 minutes, until golden brown. Remove from the oven and cool.

For the filling, place the vanilla pod in a saucepan with the milk and leave on a low heat to infuse, without boiling, for 10 minutes. Whisk the egg yolks, sugar, flour and cornflour together in a mixing bowl until smooth. Strain the milk into the bowl and whisk until smooth.

Pour the mixture back into the pan and stir over a moderate heat until boiling. Cook, stirring constantly, for about 2 minutes until thickened and smooth. Remove from the heat and fold in the whipped cream. Spoon the mixture into the pastry cases.

When the filling has set slightly, top with strawberries, sliced if large, then spoon over a little redcurrant jelly to glaze.

SERVES 8

pastry

125 g/4½ oz plain flour

2 tbsp icing sugar

70 g/2½ oz unsalted butter, at room temperature

1 egg yolk

1–2 tbsp water

filling

1 vanilla pod, split

200 ml/7 fl oz milk

2 egg yolks

40 g/1½ oz caster sugar

1 tbsp plain flour

1 tbsp cornflour

125 ml/4 fl oz double cream, softly whipped

350 g/12 oz strawberries, hulled

4 tbsp redcurrant jelly, melted

APPLE STRUDEL WITH CIDER SAUCE

Preheat the oven to 190°C/375°F/Gas Mark 5. Line a baking tray with baking paper.

Peel and core the apples and chop them into 1-cm/½-inch dice. Toss the apples in a bowl with the lemon juice, sultanas, cinnamon, nutmeg and brown sugar.

Lay out a sheet of filo pastry, spray with vegetable oil and lay a second sheet on top. Repeat with a third sheet. Spread over half the apple mixture and roll up lengthways, tucking in the ends to enclose the filling. Repeat to make a second strudel. Slide onto the baking tray, spray with oil and bake in the preheated oven for 15–20 minutes.

To make the sauce, blend the cornflour in a saucepan with a little cider until smooth. Add the remaining cider and heat gently, stirring, until the mixture boils and thickens. Serve the strudel warm or cold, dredged with icing sugar, and accompanied by the cider sauce.

SERVES 2–4

8 eating apples

1 tbsp lemon juice

115 g/4 oz sultanas

1 tsp ground cinnamon

½ tsp ground nutmeg

1 tbsp soft light brown sugar

6 sheets filo pastry, thawed, if frozen

vegetable oil spray

icing sugar, to serve

sauce

1 tbsp cornflour

450 ml/16 fl oz dry cider

BAKLAVA

MAKES 25

225 g/8 oz walnut halves

225 g/8 oz shelled
   pistachio nuts

100 g/3½ oz blanched
   almonds

4 tbsp pine kernels,
   finely chopped

Finely grated rind of
   2 large oranges

5 tbsp sesame seeds

1 tbsp sugar

½ tsp ground cinnamon

½ tsp mixed spice

23 sheets filo pastry,
   thawed, if frozen

250 g/9 oz butter, melted,
   plus extra for greasing

Syrup

450 g/1 lb caster sugar

450 ml/16 fl oz water

5 tbsp honey

3 cloves

2 large strips lemon zest

To make the filling, put the walnuts, pistachio nuts, almonds and pine kernels in a food processor and process gently, until finely chopped but not ground. Transfer the chopped nuts to a bowl and stir in the orange rind, sesame seeds, sugar, cinnamon and mixed spice.

Preheat the oven to 160°C/325°F/Gas Mark 3. Grease a 25-cm/10-inch square ovenproof dish, about 5 cm/2 inches deep. Cut the stacked filo sheets to size, using a ruler. Keep the sheets covered with a damp cloth. Place a sheet of filo on the base of the dish and brush with melted butter. Top with seven more sheets, brushing with butter between each layer.

Sprinkle with a generous 150 g/5½ oz of the filling. Top with three sheets of filo, brushing each one with butter. Continue layering until you have used up all the filo and filling, ending with a top layer of three filo sheets. Brush with butter.

Using a sharp knife cut the baklava into 5-cm/2-inch squares. Brush again with butter. Bake in the preheated oven for 1 hour.

Meanwhile, put all the syrup ingredients in a saucepan. Slowly bring to the boil, stirring to dissolve the sugar, then simmer for 15 minutes, without stirring, until a thin syrup forms. Leave to cool.

Remove the baklava from the oven and strain the syrup over the top. Leave to cool in the dish, then cut out the squares to serve.

APPLE DANISH

Place the flour in a bowl and rub in 25 g/1 oz of the butter. Chill the remaining butter in the freezer until hard but not frozen. Dust with flour and grate coarsely into a bowl. Chill. Stir the salt, yeast and sugar into the flour mixture. In another bowl, beat the egg with the vanilla extract and water, then add to the flour mixture and mix to form a dough. Knead for 10 minutes on a floured surface, then chill for 10 minutes.

Roll out the dough to 30 x 20 cm/12 x 8 inches and mark it lengthways into thirds. Sprinkle the grated butter over the top two thirds, leaving a 1–2-cm/½–¾-inch border around the edge. Fold the bottom third of dough over the centre, then fold down the top third. Give the dough a quarter turn (so the short edge is nearest you) and roll out as big as the original rectangle. Fold the bottom third up and the top third down again. Wrap and chill for 30 minutes. Repeat this rolling, folding and turning four times, chilling well each time. Finally, chill overnight.

Preheat the oven to 200°C/400°F/Gas Mark 6. Grease two baking trays. For the filling, mix the apples with the lemon rind and 3 tablespoons of the sugar. Roll out the dough into a 40-cm/16-inch square and cut into 16 squares. Pile a little of the apple filling in the centre of each square. Brush the edges with milk and fold the corners together into the centre. Place on the prepared baking trays and chill for about 15 minutes.

Brush the pastries with milk and sprinkle with the remaining sugar. Bake in the preheated oven for 10 minutes. Reduce the heat to 180°C/350°F/Gas Mark 4 and bake for a further 10–15 minutes.

MAKES 16

danish pastry dough

280 g/10 oz strong white flour, plus extra for dusting

175 g/6 oz butter, well chilled, plus extra for greasing

¼ tsp salt

7 g/¼ oz easy-blend dried yeast

2 tbsp caster sugar

1 egg, at room temperature

1 tsp vanilla extract

6 tbsp lukewarm water

milk, for glazing

filling

2 cooking apples, peeled, cored and chopped

grated rind of 1 lemon

4 tbsp sugar

DOUBLE CHOCOLATE SWIRLS

Mix together the flour, yeast, sugar, salt and cinnamon in a large bowl.

Melt the butter in a heatproof bowl set over a saucepan of gently simmering water, then allow to cool slightly. Whisk in the eggs and milk. Pour into the flour mixture and mix well to form a dough.

Turn out onto a floured work surface and knead for 10 minutes, until smooth. Put into a large floured bowl, cover with clingfilm and put in a warm place for 1½–2 hours.

When you are ready to make the buns, take the dough from the bowl and punch down. Preheat the oven to 220°C/425°F/Gas Mark 7 and lightly oil two baking trays.

Divide the dough into four pieces and roll each piece into a rectangle about 2.5 cm/1 inch thick. Spread each rectangle with the chocolate hazelnut spread and scatter with the chopped chocolate. Roll up each piece from one of the long edges, then cut into 6 pieces. Place each swirl, cut-side down, on the baking trays and brush well with the beaten egg. Bake in the preheated oven for 12–15 minutes and serve warm.

MAKES 24

600 g/1 lb 5 oz strong white flour, plus extra for dusting

7 g/¼ oz easy-blend dried yeast

115 g/4 oz caster sugar

½ tsp salt

1 tsp ground cinnamon

85 g/3 oz unsalted butter

2 large eggs, beaten, plus extra for glazing

300 ml/10 fl oz milk

oil, for greasing

filling

6 tbsp chocolate hazelnut spread

200 g/7 oz milk chocolate, chopped

CINNAMON ROLLS

MAKES 8

350 g/12 oz self-raising flour,
   plus extra for dusting

pinch of salt

1 tbsp caster sugar

1 tsp ground cinnamon

100 g/3½ oz butter, melted,
   plus extra for greasing

2 egg yolks

200 ml/7 fl oz milk,
   plus extra for glazing

Filling

1 tsp ground cinnamon

55 g/2 oz soft light brown sugar

2 tbsp caster sugar

1 tbsp butter, melted

Icing

125 g/4½ oz icing sugar, sifted

2 tbsp cream cheese,
   softened

1 tbsp butter, softened

about 2 tbsp boiling water

1 tsp vanilla extract

Preheat the oven to 180°C/350°F/Gas Mark 4. Grease a 20-cm/ 8-inch round cake tin and line the base with baking paper.

Mix the flour, salt, caster sugar and cinnamon together in a large bowl. Whisk the butter, egg yolks and milk together and combine with the dry ingredients to make a soft dough. Turn out onto a large piece of baking paper lightly sprinkled with flour, and roll out to a rectangle measuring 30 x 25 cm/ 12 x 10 inches.

To make the filling, mix the ingredients together, spread evenly over the dough and roll up, Swiss-roll style, to form a log. Using a sharp knife, cut the dough into eight even-sized slices and pack into the prepared tin. Brush gently with extra milk and bake in the preheated oven for 30–35 minutes, or until golden brown. Remove from the oven and leave to cool for 5 minutes before removing from the tin.

Sift the icing sugar into a large bowl and make a well in the centre. Place the cream cheese and butter in the centre, pour over the water and stir to mix. Add extra boiling water, a few drops at a time, until the icing coats the back of a spoon. Stir in the vanilla extract. Drizzle over the rolls. Serve warm or cold.

CROWN LOAF

Grease a baking tray. Sift the flour and salt into a bowl. Stir in the yeast. Rub in the butter with your fingertips. Add the milk and egg and mix to form a dough.

Place the dough in a greased bowl, cover and stand in a warm place for 40 minutes, until doubled in size. Punch down the dough lightly for 1 minute. Roll out to a rectangle measuring about 30 x 23 cm/12 x 9 inches.

To make the filling, cream together the butter and sugar until light and fluffy. Stir in the hazelnuts, ginger, mixed peel and rum. Spread the filling over the dough, leaving a 2.5-cm/1-inch border.

Roll up the dough, starting from one of the long edges, into a sausage shape. Cut into slices at 5-cm/2-inch intervals and place, cut-side down, in a circle on the prepared baking tray with the slices just touching. Cover and stand in a warm place to prove for 30 minutes.

Preheat the oven to 190°C/375°F/Gas Mark 5. Bake the loaf for 20–30 minutes, or until golden. Meanwhile, mix the icing sugar with enough lemon juice to form a thin icing.

Leave the loaf to cool slightly before drizzling with the icing. Leave the icing to set before serving.

SERVES 6

225 g/8 oz strong white flour

½ tsp salt

7 g/¼ oz easy-blend dried yeast

2 tbsp butter, diced, plus extra for greasing

125 ml/4 fl oz tepid milk

1 egg, lightly beaten

filling

4 tbsp butter, softened

50 g/1¾ oz soft light brown sugar

2 tbsp chopped hazelnuts

1 tbsp chopped stem ginger

50 g/1¾ oz chopped mixed peel

1 tbsp dark rum or brandy

icing

115 g/4 oz icing sugar

1–2 tbsp lemon juice

FRESH CROISSANTS

Preheat the oven to 200°C/400°F/Gas Mark 6. Stir the dry ingredients into a large bowl, make a well in the centre and add the milk. Mix to a soft dough, adding more milk if too dry. Knead on a lightly floured work surface for 5–10 minutes, or until smooth and elastic. Place in a large greased bowl, cover, and leave in a warm place until doubled in size. Meanwhile, place the butter between two sheets of baking paper and flatten with a rolling pin to form a rectangle about 5 mm/¼ inch thick. Chill.

Knead the dough for 1 minute. Remove the butter from the refrigerator and leave to soften slightly. Roll out the dough on a well-floured work surface to 46 x 15 cm/18 x 6 inches. Place the butter in the centre, folding up the sides and squeezing the edges together gently. With the short end of the dough towards you, fold the top third down towards the centre, then fold the bottom third up. Give the dough a quarter turn, roll out as big as the original rectangle and fold again. If the butter feels soft, wrap the dough in clingfilm and chill. Repeat the rolling process twice more. Cut the dough in half. Roll out each half into a rectangle 5 mm/¼ inch thick. Use a cardboard triangular template, base 18 cm/7 inches and sides 20 cm/8 inches, to cut out the croissants.

Brush the triangles lightly with the glaze. Roll into croissant shapes, starting at the base and tucking the point underneath to prevent the croissants from unrolling while cooking. Brush again with the glaze. Place on a baking tray and leave to double in size. Bake in the preheated oven for 15–20 minutes, until golden brown.

MAKES 12

500 g/1 lb 2 oz strong white flour, plus extra for dusting

40 g/1½ oz caster sugar

1 tsp salt

2 tsp easy-blend dried yeast

300 ml/10 fl oz lukewarm milk

300 g/10½ oz butter, softened, plus extra for greasing

1 egg, lightly beaten with 1 tbsp milk, for glazing

PAIN AU CHOCOLAT

MAKES 12

175 g/6 oz butter, softened,
  plus extra for greasing

500 g/1 lb 2 oz strong white flour

½ tsp salt

7 g/¼ oz easy-blend dried yeast

2 tbsp lard or white vegetable fat

1 egg, lightly beaten

225 ml/8 fl oz tepid water

100 g/3½ oz plain chocolate,
  broken into 12 squares

beaten egg, for glazing

Lightly grease a baking tray. Sift the flour and salt into a bowl and stir in the yeast. Rub in the lard with your fingertips. Add the egg and enough of the water to mix to a soft dough. Knead for about 10 minutes to make a smooth elastic dough.

Roll out to a 38 x 20-cm/15 x 8-inch rectangle and mark it vertically into thirds. Divide the butter into three portions and dot one portion over the first two thirds of the rectangle, leaving a small border around the edge.

Fold the rectangle into three by first folding over the plain part of the dough and then folding over the other side. Seal the edges of the dough by pressing with a rolling pin. Give the dough a quarter turn and roll out as big as the original rectangle. Fold again (without adding butter), then wrap the dough and chill for 30 minutes.

Repeat this rolling, folding and turning twice more until all of the butter has been used, chilling the dough each time. Re-roll and fold twice more without butter. Chill for a final 30 minutes.

Roll out the dough to 45 x 30 cm/18 x 12 inches and halve lengthways. Cut each half into six rectangles and brush with beaten egg. Place a chocolate square at one end of each rectangle and roll up to form a sausage. Press the ends together and place, seam-side down, on the prepared baking tray. Cover and leave to prove for 40 minutes in a warm place. Preheat the oven to 220°C/425°F/Gas Mark 7. Brush each pastry roll with egg and bake in the preheated oven for 20–25 minutes, until golden. Cool on a wire rack. Serve warm or cold.

CHOCOLATE ÉCLAIRS

Preheat the oven to 200°C/400°F/Gas Mark 6. Lightly grease a baking tray.

Place the water in a saucepan, add the butter and heat gently until the butter melts. Bring to a rolling boil, then remove the saucepan from the heat and add the flour all at once, beating well until the mixture leaves the sides of the saucepan and forms a ball. Leave to cool slightly, then gradually beat in the eggs to form a smooth, glossy mixture. Spoon into a large piping bag fitted with a 1-cm/½-inch plain nozzle.

Sprinkle the baking tray with a little water. Pipe éclairs 7.5 cm/ 3 inches long, spaced well apart. Bake in the preheated oven for 30–35 minutes, or until crisp and golden. Make a small slit in the side of each éclair, then leave to cool on a wire rack.

Meanwhile, make the pastry cream. Whisk the eggs and caster sugar until thick and creamy, then fold in the cornflour. Heat the milk until almost boiling and pour onto the egg mixture, whisking. Transfer to the saucepan and cook over a low heat, stirring until thick. Remove the saucepan from the heat and stir in the vanilla extract. Cover and leave to cool.

To make the icing, melt the butter with the milk in a saucepan, remove from the heat and stir in the cocoa and icing sugar. Split the éclairs lengthways and pipe in the pastry cream. Spread the icing over the top of the éclairs. Melt a little white chocolate in a heatproof bowl set over a saucepan of gently simmering water, then drizzle over the chocolate icing and leave to set.

MAKES 12

choux pastry
150 ml/5 fl oz water

70 g/2½ oz butter, diced, plus extra for greasing

100 g/3½ oz plain flour, sifted

2 eggs

pastry cream
2 eggs, lightly beaten

4 tbsp caster sugar

2 tbsp cornflour

300 ml/10 fl oz milk

¼ tsp vanilla extract

icing
2 tbsp butter

1 tbsp milk

1 tbsp cocoa powder

55 g/2 oz icing sugar

50 g/1¾ oz white chocolate, broken into pieces

STRAWBERRY PETITS CHOUX

Sprinkle the gelatine over the water in a heatproof bowl. Let it soften for 2 minutes. Place the bowl over a saucepan of simmering water and stir until the gelatine dissolves. Remove from the heat.

Place 225 g/8 oz of the strawberries in a blender with the ricotta, sugar and liqueur. Process until blended. Add the gelatine and process briefly. Transfer the mousse to a bowl, cover with clingfilm and chill for 1–1½ hours, until set.

Preheat the oven to 220°C/425°F/Gas Mark 7. Line a baking tray with baking paper.

To make the petits choux, sift together the flour, cocoa powder and salt. Put the butter and water into a heavy-based saucepan and heat gently until the butter has melted. Remove the saucepan from the heat and add the flour mixture all at once, stirring well until the mixture leaves the sides of the saucepan. Leave to cool slightly.

Gradually beat the eggs and egg white into the flour paste and continue beating until it is smooth and glossy. Drop 12 rounded tablespoonfuls of the mixture onto the prepared baking tray and bake in the preheated oven for 20–25 minutes, until puffed up and crisp. Remove from the oven and make a slit in the side of each petit chou. Return to the oven for 5 minutes. Transfer to a wire rack.

Slice the remaining strawberries. Cut the petits choux in half, divide the mousse and strawberry slices between them, then replace the tops. Dust lightly with icing sugar and place in the refrigerator. Serve within 1½ hours.

MAKES 12

filling and topping

2 tsp powdered gelatine

2 tbsp water

350 g/12 oz strawberries

225 g/8 oz ricotta cheese

1 tbsp caster sugar

2 tsp crème de fraises de bois

icing sugar, for dusting

petits choux

100 g/3½ oz plain flour

2 tbsp cocoa powder

pinch of salt

6 tbsp unsalted butter

225 ml/8 fl oz water

2 eggs, plus 1 egg white, beaten

PROFITEROLES & CHOCOLATE SAUCE

SERVES 4

choux pastry

200 ml/7 fl oz water

70 g/2½ oz butter, plus extra
for greasing

100 g/3½ oz plain flour, sifted

3 eggs, beaten

cream filling

300 ml/10 fl oz double cream

3 tbsp caster sugar

1 tsp vanilla extract

chocolate sauce

125 g/4½ oz plain chocolate,
broken into small pieces

35 g/1¼ oz butter

6 tbsp water

2 tbsp brandy

Preheat the oven to 200°C/400°F/Gas Mark 6. Grease a large
baking tray.

To make the choux pastry, put the water and butter into
a saucepan and bring to the boil. Immediately add all the
flour, remove the pan from the heat and stir the mixture into
a paste that leaves the sides of the pan clean. Leave to cool
slightly. Beat in enough of the eggs to give the mixture a soft
dropping consistency.

Transfer to a piping bag fitted with a 1-cm/½-inch plain nozzle.
Pipe small balls onto the prepared baking tray. Bake in the
preheated oven for 25 minutes. Remove from the oven. Pierce each
ball with a skewer to allow the steam to escape.

To make the filling, whip together the cream, sugar and vanilla
extract. Cut the pastry balls almost in half, then fill with cream.

To make the sauce, gently melt the chocolate and butter with
the water in a heatproof bowl set over a saucepan of gently
simmering water, stirring until smooth. Stir in the brandy. Pile the
profiteroles into individual serving dishes or into a pyramid on a
raised cake stand. Pour over the sauce and serve.

BISCUITS

CHOCOLATE
CHIP COOKIES

Preheat the oven to 190ºC/375ºF/Gas Mark 5. Lightly grease two baking trays.

   Place all of the ingredients in a large mixing bowl and beat until well combined.

   Place tablespoonfuls of the mixture onto the prepared baking trays, spacing them well apart to allow for spreading during cooking.

   Bake in the preheated oven for 10–12 minutes, or until the cookies are golden brown.

   Using a palette knife, transfer the cookies to a wire rack to cool completely.

MAKES 30

unsalted butter, for greasing

175 g/6 oz plain flour

1 tsp baking powder

125 g/4½ oz soft margarine

85 g/3 oz light muscovado sugar

55 g/2 oz caster sugar

½ tsp vanilla extract

1 egg

125 g/4½ oz plain chocolate chips

MEGA CHIP COOKIES

Preheat the oven to 190°C/375°F/Gas Mark 5. Line two to three baking trays with baking paper.

Put the butter and sugar into a bowl and mix well with a wooden spoon, then beat in the egg yolk and vanilla extract. Sift together the flour, cocoa powder and salt into the mixture, add both kinds of chocolate chips and stir until thoroughly combined.

Make 12 balls of the mixture, put them onto the prepared baking trays, spaced well apart, and flatten slightly. Press the pieces of plain chocolate into the cookies.

Bake in the preheated oven for 12–15 minutes. Leave to cool on the baking trays for 5–10 minutes, then, using a palette knife carefully transfer to wire racks to cool completely.

MAKES 12

225 g/8 oz butter, softened

140 g/5 oz caster sugar

1 egg yolk, lightly beaten

2 tsp vanilla extract

225 g/8 oz plain flour

55 g/2 oz cocoa powder

pinch of salt

85 g/3 oz milk chocolate chips

85 g/3 oz white chocolate chips

115 g/4 oz plain chocolate, roughly chopped

CLASSIC OATMEAL BISCUITS

MAKES 30

175 g/6 oz butter or margarine,
  plus extra for greasing

275 g/9¾ oz demerara sugar

1 egg

1 tbsp water

1 tsp vanilla extract

375 g/13 oz rolled oats

140 g/5 oz plain flour

1 tsp salt

½ tsp bicarbonate of soda

Preheat the oven to 350°F/180°C/Gas Mark 4 and grease a large baking tray.

Cream the butter and sugar together in a large mixing bowl. Beat in the egg, water and vanilla extract until the mixture is smooth. In a separate bowl, mix the oats, flour, salt and bicarbonate of soda.

Gradually stir the oat mixture into the creamed mixture until thoroughly combined.

Place tablespoonfuls of the mixture onto the prepared baking tray, making sure they are well spaced. Transfer to the preheated oven and bake for 15 minutes, or until the biscuits are golden brown.

Remove the bscuits from the oven and place on a wire rack to cool before serving.

TRADITIONAL EASTER BISCUITS

Put the butter and sugar into a bowl and mix well with a wooden spoon, then beat in the egg yolk. Sift together the flour, mixed spice and a pinch of salt into the mixture, add the mixed peel and currants and stir until thoroughly combined. Halve the dough, shape into balls, wrap in clingfilm and chill in the refrigerator for 30–60 minutes.

Preheat the oven to 190°C/375°F/Gas Mark 5. Line two baking trays with baking paper.

Unwrap the dough and roll out between two sheets of baking paper. Stamp out rounds with a 6-cm/2½-inch fluted biscuit cutter and put them on the prepared baking trays, spaced well apart.

Bake in the preheated oven for 7 minutes, then brush with the egg white and sprinkle with caster sugar. Return to the oven and bake for a further 5–8 minutes, until light golden brown. Leave to cool on the baking trays for 5–10 minutes, then, using a palette knife, carefully transfer to wire racks to cool completely.

BISCUITS

224

MAKES ABOUT 30

225 g/8 oz butter, softened

140 g/5 oz caster sugar, plus extra for sprinkling

1 egg yolk, lightly beaten

280 g/10 oz plain flour

1 tsp mixed spice

pinch of salt

1 tbsp chopped mixed peel

55 g/2 oz currants

1 egg white, lightly beaten

PEANUT BUTTER
COOKIES

Preheat the oven to 180°C/350°F/Gas Mark 4, then grease three
baking trays.

Place the butter and peanut butter in a bowl and beat together.
Beat in the caster sugar and muscovado sugar, then gradually
beat in the egg and the vanilla extract.

Sift the flour, bicarbonate of soda, baking powder and salt into
the mixture, add the oats and stir until just combined.

Place spoonfuls of the mixture onto the prepared baking trays,
spaced well apart to allow for spreading. Flatten slightly with
a fork.

Bake in the preheated oven for 12 minutes, or until lightly
browned. Leave to cool on the baking trays for 2 minutes, then
transfer to wire racks to cool completely.

MAKES 26

115 g/4 oz butter, softened,
   plus extra for greasing

115 g/4 oz crunchy peanut butter

115 g/4 oz golden caster sugar

115 g/4 oz light muscovado sugar

1 egg, beaten

½ tsp vanilla extract

85 g/3 oz plain flour

½ tsp bicarbonate of soda

½ tsp baking powder

pinch of salt

115 g/4 oz rolled oats

SNICKERDOODLES

MAKES ABOUT 40

225 g/8 oz butter, softened

140 g/5 oz caster sugar

2 large eggs, lightly beaten

1 tsp vanilla extract

400 g/14 oz plain flour

1 tsp bicarbonate of soda

1/2 tsp freshly grated nutmeg

pinch of salt

55 g/2 oz pecan nuts, finely
chopped

cinnamon coating

2 tbsp caster sugar

2 tbsp ground cinnamon

Put the butter and sugar into a bowl and mix well with a wooden spoon, then beat in the eggs and vanilla extract. Sift together the flour, bicarbonate of soda, nutmeg and salt into the mixture, add the pecan nuts and stir until thoroughly combined. Shape the dough into a ball, wrap in clingfilm and chill in the refrigerator for 30–60 minutes.

Preheat the oven to 190°C/375°F/Gas Mark 5. Line two baking trays with baking paper.

For the cinnamon coating, mix together the caster sugar and cinnamon in a shallow dish. Scoop up tablespoons of the cookie dough and roll into balls. Roll each ball in the cinnamon mixture to coat and place on the prepared baking trays, spaced well apart.

Bake in the preheated oven for 10–12 minutes, until golden brown. Leave to cool on the baking trays for 5–10 minutes, then, using a palette knife, carefully transfer to wire racks to cool completely.

GINGERSNAPS

Preheat the oven to 160°C/325°F/Gas Mark 3, then lightly grease
several baking trays.

Sift together the flour, salt, sugar, ginger and bicarbonate of
soda into a large mixing bowl.

Heat the butter and golden syrup together in a saucepan over
a very low heat until the butter has melted. Remove the pan from
the heat and leave to cool slightly, then pour the contents onto
the dry ingredients.

Add the egg and orange rind and mix thoroughly to form a
dough. Using your hands, carefully shape the dough into
30 even-sized balls.

Place the balls well apart on the prepared baking trays, then
flatten them slightly with your fingers.

Bake in the preheated oven for 15–20 minutes, then carefully
transfer to a wire rack to cool.

MAKES 30

350 g/12 oz self-raising flour

pinch of salt

200 g/7 oz caster sugar

1 tbsp ground ginger

1 tsp bicarbonate of soda

125 g/4½ oz butter, plus extra
for greasing

75 g/2¾ oz golden syrup

1 egg, beaten

1 tsp grated orange rind

SHORTBREAD

Preheat the oven to 150°C/300°F/Gas Mark 2. Grease a 20-cm/ 8-inch fluted round tart tin.

Mix together the flour, salt and sugar. Rub the butter into the dry ingredients. Continue to work the mixture until it forms a soft dough. Make sure you do not overwork the shortbread or it will be tough, not crumbly as it should be.

Lightly press the dough into the prepared tart tin. If you don't have a fluted tin, roll out the dough on a lightly floured board, place on a baking tray and pinch the edges to form a scalloped pattern.

Mark into eight pieces with a knife. Prick all over with a fork and bake in the preheated oven for 45–50 minutes, until the shortbread is firm and just coloured.

Leave to cool in the tin and sprinkle with the sugar. Cut into portions and remove to a wire rack to cool.

MAKES 8

175 g/6 oz plain flour, plus extra for dusting

pinch of salt

55 g/2 oz caster sugar, plus extra for sprinkling

115 g/4 oz butter, cut into small pieces, plus extra for greasing

CITRUS CRESCENTS

MAKES ABOUT 25

100 g/3½ oz butter, softened, plus extra for greasing

75 g/2¾ oz caster sugar

1 egg, separated

200 g/7 oz plain flour, plus extra for dusting

grated rind of 1 orange

grated rind of 1 lemon

grated rind of 1 lime

2–3 tbsp orange juice

Preheat the oven to 200°C/400°F/Gas Mark 6. Lightly grease two baking trays.

In a mixing bowl, cream together the butter and sugar until light and fluffy, then gradually beat in the egg yolk.

Sift the flour into the creamed mixture and mix until evenly combined. Add the orange, lemon and lime rinds to the mixture with enough of the orange juice to make a soft dough.

Roll out the dough on a lightly floured surface. Stamp out rounds using a 7.5-cm/3-inch biscuit cutter. Make crescent shapes by cutting away a quarter of each round. Re-roll the trimmings to make about 25 crescents.

Place the crescents on the prepared baking trays. Prick the surface of each crescent with a fork. Lightly whisk the egg white in a small bowl and brush it over the biscuits.

Bake in the preheated oven for 12–15 minutes. Leave the biscuits to cool on a wire rack before serving.

VANILLA HEARTS

Preheat the oven to 180ºC/350ºF/Gas Mark 4, then lightly grease a baking tray.

Sift the flour into a large bowl. Add the butter and rub it in with your fingertips until the mixture resembles fine breadcrumbs. Stir in the sugar and vanilla extract and mix together to form a firm dough.

Roll out the dough on a lightly floured work surface to a thickness of 1 cm/½ inch. Stamp out 12 hearts with a heart-shaped biscuit cutter measuring about 5 cm/2 inches across. Arrange the hearts on the prepared baking tray.

Bake in the preheated oven for 15–20 minutes, or until just coloured. Transfer to a wire rack and leave to cool completely. Dust with a little caster sugar just before serving.

MAKES 12

225 g/8 oz plain flour, plus extra for dusting

150 g/5½ oz butter, cut into small pieces, plus extra for greasing

125 g/4½ oz caster sugar, plus extra for dusting

1 tsp vanilla extract

JAM RINGS

Put the butter and caster sugar into a bowl and mix well with a wooden spoon, then beat in the egg yolk and vanilla extract. Sift together the flour and salt into the mixture and stir until thoroughly combined. Halve the dough, shape into balls, wrap in clingfilm and chill in the refrigerator for 30–60 minutes.

Preheat the oven to 190ºC/375ºF/Gas Mark 5. Line two baking trays with baking paper.

Unwrap the dough and roll out between two sheets of baking paper. Stamp out biscuits with a 7-cm/2¾-inch fluted round cutter and put half of them on one of the prepared baking trays, spaced well apart. Using a 4-cm/1½-inch plain round cutter, stamp out the centres of the remaining biscuits and remove. Put the rings on the other baking tray, spaced well apart.

Bake in the preheated oven for 7 minutes, then brush the biscuit rings with beaten egg white and sprinkle with caster sugar. Bake for a further 5–8 minutes, until light golden brown. Leave to cool on the baking trays for 5–10 minutes, then, using a palette knife, carefully transfer to wire racks to cool completely.

To make the jam filling, beat the butter and icing sugar together in a bowl until smooth and combined. Spread the filling over the whole biscuits and top with a little jam. Place the rings on top and press gently together.

MAKES ABOUT 15

225 g/8 oz butter, softened

140 g/5 oz caster sugar, plus extra for sprinkling

1 egg yolk, lightly beaten

2 tsp vanilla extract

280 g/10 oz plain flour

pinch of salt

1 egg white, lightly beaten

filling

55 g/2 oz butter, softened

100 g/3½ oz icing sugar

5 tbsp strawberry or raspberry jam, warmed

GINGERBREAD PEOPLE

MAKES 20

450 g/1 lb plain flour, plus extra
  for dusting

2 tsp ground ginger

1 tsp ground mixed spice

2 tsp bicarbonate of soda

115 g/4 oz butter, plus extra
  for greasing

100 g/3½ oz golden syrup

115 g/4 oz light muscovado sugar

1 egg, beaten

to decorate

currants

glacé cherries

85 g/3 oz icing sugar

3–4 tsp water

Preheat the oven to 160°C/325°F/Gas Mark 3, then grease
three large baking trays.

Sift the flour, ginger, mixed spice and bicarbonate of soda into
a large bowl. Place the butter, golden syrup and muscovado
sugar in a saucepan over a low heat and stir until melted. Pour
onto the dry ingredients and add the egg. Mix together to make
a dough. The dough will be sticky to start with, but will become
firmer as it cools.

On a lightly floured work surface, roll out the dough to about
3 mm/⅛ inch thick and stamp out gingerbread people shapes.
Place on the prepared baking trays. Re-knead and re-roll the
trimmings and cut out more shapes. Decorate with currants
for eyes and pieces of glacé cherry for mouths. Bake in the
preheated oven for 15–20 minutes, or until firm and lightly
browned.

Remove from the oven and leave to cool on the baking trays for
a few minutes, then transfer to wire racks to cool completely.

Mix the icing sugar with the water to a thick consistency. Place
the icing in a small piping bag fitted with a plain nozzle and use
to pipe buttons or bows onto the cooled biscuits.

CHOCOLATE DOMINOES

Put the butter and sugar into a bowl and mix well with a wooden spoon, then beat in the egg yolk and vanilla extract. Sift together the flour, cocoa powder and a pinch of salt into the mixture, add the coconut and stir until thoroughly combined. Halve the dough, shape into balls, wrap in clingfilm and chill in the refrigerator for 30–60 minutes.

Preheat the oven to 190°C/375°F/Gas Mark 5. Line two baking trays with baking paper.

Unwrap the dough and roll out between two sheets of baking paper. Stamp out biscuits with a 9-cm/3½-inch plain square cutter, then cut them in half to make rectangles. Put them on the prepared baking trays and, using a knife, make a line across the centre of each without cutting through. Arrange the chocolate chips on top of the biscuits to look like dominoes, pressing them in gently.

Bake in the preheated oven for 10–15 minutes, until golden brown. Leave to cool on the baking trays for 5–10 minutes, then, using a palette knife, carefully transfer to wire racks to cool completely.

MAKES 28

225 g/8 oz butter, softened

140 g/5 oz caster sugar

1 egg yolk, lightly beaten

2 tsp vanilla extract

250 g/9 oz plain flour

25 g/1 oz cocoa powder

pinch of salt

25 g/1 oz desiccated coconut

50 g/1¾ oz white chocolate chips

CHEQUERBOARD COOKIES

Put the butter and sugar into a bowl and mix well with a wooden spoon, then beat in the egg yolk and vanilla extract. Sift together the flour and salt into the mixture and stir until thoroughly combined.

Divide the dough in half. Add the ginger and orange rind to one half and mix well. Shape the dough into a log 15 cm/ 6 inches long. Flatten the sides and top to square off the log to 5 cm/2 inches high. Wrap in clingfilm and chill in the refrigerator for 30–60 minutes. Add the cocoa to the other half of the dough and mix well. Shape into a flattened log exactly the same size as the first one, wrap in clingfilm and chill in the refrigerator for 30–60 minutes.

Unwrap the dough and cut each flattened log lengthways into three slices. Cut each slice lengthways into three strips. Brush the strips with egg white and stack them in threes, alternating the colours, so they are the same shape as the original logs. Wrap in clingfilm and chill in the refrigerator for 30–60 minutes.

Preheat the oven to 190°C/375°F/Gas Mark 5. Line two baking trays with baking paper.

Unwrap the logs and cut into slices with a sharp serrated knife. Put the cookies on the prepared baking trays, spaced well apart. Bake in the preheated oven for 12–15 minutes, until firm. Leave to cool for 5–10 minutes, then carefully transfer to wire racks to cool completely.

MAKES ABOUT 20

225 g/8 oz butter, softened

140 g/5 oz caster sugar

1 egg yolk, lightly beaten

2 tsp vanilla extract

280 g/10 oz plain flour

pinch of salt

1 tsp ground ginger

1 tbsp finely grated orange rind

1 tbsp cocoa powder, sifted

1 egg white, lightly beaten

CHOCOLATE COOKIE SANDWICHES

MAKES ABOUT 15

225 g/8 oz butter, softened

140 g/5 oz caster sugar

2 tsp finely grated orange rind

1 egg yolk, lightly beaten

2 tsp vanilla extract

250 g/9 oz plain flour

25 g/1 oz cocoa powder

pinch of salt

100 g/3½ oz plain chocolate, finely chopped

chocolate filling

125 ml/4 fl oz double cream

200 g/7 oz white chocolate, broken into pieces

1 tsp orange extract

Preheat the oven to 190°C/375°F/Gas Mark 5. Line two baking trays with baking paper.

Put the butter, sugar and orange rind into a bowl and mix well with a wooden spoon, then beat in the egg yolk and vanilla extract. Sift together the flour, cocoa powder and salt into the mixture, add the chopped chocolate and stir until thoroughly combined.

Scoop up tablespoons of the dough, roll into balls and place on the prepared baking trays, spaced well apart. Gently flatten and smooth the tops with the back of a spoon.

Bake in the preheated oven for 10–15 minutes, until light golden brown. Leave to cool on the baking trays for 5–10 minutes, then, using a palette knife, carefully transfer to wire racks to cool completely.

To make the filling, bring the cream to the boil in a small saucepan, then remove the pan from the heat. Stir in the chocolate until the mixture is smooth, then stir in the orange extract. When the mixture is completely cool, use to sandwich the cookies together in pairs.

CHOCOLATE MINT COOKIE SANDWICHES

Put the butter and sugar into a bowl and mix well with a wooden spoon, then beat in the egg yolk and vanilla extract. Sift together the flour, cocoa powder and salt into the mixture, add the cherries and stir until thoroughly combined. Halve the dough, shape into balls, wrap in clingfilm and chill in the refrigerator for 30–60 minutes.

Preheat the oven to 190°C/375°F/Gas Mark 5. Line two baking trays with baking paper.

Unwrap the dough and roll out between two sheets of baking paper. Stamp out cookies with a 6-cm/2½-inch plain square cutter and put them on the prepared baking trays, spaced well apart.

Bake in the preheated oven for 10–15 minutes, until firm. Immediately place an after-dinner mint on top of half of the cookies, then cover with the remaining cookies. Press down gently and leave to cool on the baking trays.

Melt the plain chocolate in a heatproof bowl set over a saucepan of gently simmering water. Remove from the heat and leave to cool. Put the cookies on a wire rack over a sheet of baking paper. Spoon the plain chocolate over them, then tap the rack to level the surface and leave to set. Melt the white chocolate in a heatproof bowl set over a pan of barely simmering water. Remove from the heat and leave to cool. Pipe or drizzle it over the cookies, then leave to set.

MAKES ABOUT 15

225 g/8 oz butter, softened

140 g/5 oz caster sugar

1 egg yolk, lightly beaten

2 tsp vanilla extract

250 g/9 oz plain flour

25 g/1 oz cocoa powder

pinch of salt

55 g/2 oz glacé cherries, finely chopped

15 after-dinner mint thins

chocolate topping

115 g/4 oz plain chocolate, broken into pieces

55 g/2 oz white chocolate, broken into pieces

ICED CHERRY RINGS

Preheat the oven to 200°C/400°F/Gas Mark 6. Lightly grease two baking trays.

Cream together the butter and caster sugar until pale and fluffy. Beat in the egg yolk and lemon rind. Sift in the flour, stir, then add the glacé cherries, mixing with your hands to a soft dough.

Roll out the dough on a lightly floured surface to about 5 mm/¼ inch thick. Stamp out 8-cm/3¼-inch rounds with a biscuit cutter. Stamp out the centre of each with a 2.5-cm/1-inch cutter and place the rings on the prepared baking trays. Re-roll any trimmings and cut more biscuits.

Bake in the preheated oven for 12–15 minutes, until firm and golden brown.

Allow to cool on the baking trays for 2 minutes, then transfer to a wire rack to finish cooling.

Mix the icing sugar to a smooth paste with the lemon juice. Drizzle over the biscuits and leave until set.

MAKES ABOUT 18

115 g/4 oz unsalted butter, plus extra for greasing

85 g/3 oz golden caster sugar

1 egg yolk

finely grated rind of ½ lemon

200 g/7 oz plain flour, plus extra for dusting

55 g/2 oz glacé cherries, finely chopped

icing

85 g/3 oz icing sugar

1½ tbsp lemon juice

VIENNESE FINGERS

MAKES ABOUT 16

100 g/3½ oz unsalted butter, plus extra for greasing

25 g/1 oz golden caster sugar

½ tsp vanilla extract

100 g/3½ oz self-raising flour

100 g/3½ oz plain chocolate

Preheat the oven to 160°C/325°F/Gas Mark 3. Lightly grease two baking trays.

Place the butter, sugar and vanilla extract in a bowl and cream together until pale and fluffy. Stir in the flour, mixing evenly to a fairly stiff dough.

Place the mixture in a piping bag fitted with a large star nozzle and pipe about 16 fingers, each 6 cm/2½ inches long, onto the prepared baking trays.

Bake in the preheated oven for 10–15 minutes, until pale golden. Cool for 2–3 minutes on the baking trays, then lift carefully onto a cooling rack with a palette knife to finish cooling.

Place the chocolate in a small heatproof bowl over a pan of gently simmering water until melted. Remove from the heat. Dip the ends of each biscuit into the chocolate to coat, then place on a sheet of baking paper and leave to set.

BRANDY SNAPS

Preheat the oven to 160°C/325°F/Gas Mark 3. Line three large baking trays with baking paper.

Place the butter, sugar and golden syrup in a saucepan and heat gently over a low heat, stirring occasionally, until melted. Remove from the heat and leave to cool slightly. Sift the flour and ginger into the pan and beat until smooth, then stir in the brandy and lemon rind.

Drop small spoonfuls of the mixture onto the prepared baking trays, leaving plenty of room for spreading. Place one baking tray at a time in the preheated oven for 10–12 minutes, or until the snaps are golden brown.

Remove the first baking tray from the oven and leave to cool for about 30 seconds, then lift each round with a palette knife and wrap around the handle of a wooden spoon. If the brandy snaps start to become too firm to wrap, return them to the oven for about 30 seconds to soften again. When firm, remove from the spoon handles and finish cooling on a wire rack. Repeat with the remaining baking trays.

For the filling, whip the cream with the brandy and icing sugar until thick. Just before serving, pipe the cream mixture into each end of the brandy snaps.

MAKES ABOUT 20

85 g/3 oz unsalted butter

85 g/3 oz golden caster sugar

3 tbsp golden syrup

85 g/3 oz plain flour

1 tsp ground ginger

1 tbsp brandy

finely grated rind of ½ lemon

filling

150 ml/5 fl oz double cream or whipping cream

1 tbsp brandy (optional)

1 tbsp icing sugar

PISTACHIO & ALMOND TUILES

Preheat the oven to 160°C/325°F/Gas Mark 3. Line two baking trays with baking paper.

Whisk the egg white lightly with the sugar, then stir in the flour, pistachios, ground almonds, almond extract and butter, mixing to a soft paste.

Place walnut-sized spoonfuls of the mixture on the prepared baking trays and use the back of the spoon to spread as thinly as possible. Bake in the preheated oven for 10–15 minutes, until pale golden.

Quickly lift each biscuit with a palette knife and place over the side of a rolling pin to shape into a curve. When set, transfer to a wire rack to cool.

MAKES 12

1 egg white

55 g/2 oz golden caster sugar

25 g/1 oz plain flour

25 g/1 oz pistachio nuts, finely chopped

25 g/1 oz ground almonds

½ tsp almond extract

40 g/1½ oz unsalted butter, melted and cooled

MINI FLORENTINES

MAKES 40

75 g/2¾ oz butter

75 g/2¾ oz caster sugar

25 g/1 oz sultanas or raisins

25 g/1 oz glacé cherries, chopped

25 g/1 oz glacé ginger, chopped

25 g/1 oz sunflower seeds

100 g/3½ oz flaked almonds

2 tbsp double cream

175 g/6 oz plain or milk chocolate, broken into pieces

Preheat the oven to 180°C/350°F/Gas Mark 4. Line two baking trays with baking paper.

Place the butter in a small saucepan and heat gently until melted. Add the sugar, stir until dissolved, then bring the mixture to the boil. Remove from the heat and stir in the sultanas, glacé cherries, glacé ginger, sunflower seeds and almonds. Mix well, then beat in the cream.

Place small teaspoons of mixture onto the prepared baking trays, allowing plenty of space for the mixture to spread during baking. Bake in the preheated oven for 10–12 minutes, or until light golden in colour.

Remove from the oven and, while still hot, use a round biscuit cutter to pull in the edges to form perfect circles. Leave to cool and go crisp before removing from the baking trays.

Put the chocolate in a heatproof bowl set over a saucepan of gently simmering water and stir until melted. Spread most of the chocolate onto a sheet of baking paper. When the chocolate is on the point of setting, place the biscuits flat-side down on the chocolate and let it harden completely.

Cut around the florentines and remove from the baking paper. Spread the remaining melted chocolate on the coated side of the florentines and use a fork to mark waves in the chocolate. Leave to set.

ALMOND BISCOTTI

Preheat the oven to 180°C/350°F/Gas Mark 4, then lightly dust a baking tray with flour.

Sift the flour, baking powder and salt into a bowl. Add the sugar, eggs and orange rind and mix to a dough. Knead in the almonds.

Roll the dough into a ball, cut in half and roll out each portion into a log about 4 cm/1½ inches in diameter. Place the logs on the prepared baking tray and then bake in the preheated oven for 10 minutes. Remove from the oven and leave to cool for 5 minutes.

Using a serrated knife, cut the logs into 1 cm/½ inch thick diagonal slices. Arrange the slices on the baking tray and return to the oven for 15 minutes, or until slightly golden. Transfer to a wire rack to cool and go crisp.

MAKES 20–24

250 g/9 oz plain flour, plus extra for dusting

1 tsp baking powder

pinch of salt

150 g/5½ oz golden caster sugar

2 eggs, beaten

finely grated rind of 1 orange

100 g/3½ oz whole blanched almonds, lightly toasted

LADIES KISSES

Cream the butter and sugar together until pale and fluffy. Beat in the egg yolk, then beat in the ground almonds and flour. Continue beating until thoroughly mixed. Shape the dough into a ball, wrap in clingfilm and chill in the refrigerator for 1½–2 hours.

Preheat the oven to 160°C/325°F/Gas Mark 3. Line three baking trays with baking paper.

Unwrap the dough, break off walnut-sized pieces and roll them into balls between the palms of your hands. Place the dough balls on the prepared baking trays, allowing space for the biscuits to spread during cooking. Bake in the preheated oven for 20–25 minutes, until golden. Carefully transfer the biscuits to wire racks to cool.

Melt the chocolate in a heatproof bowl set over a saucepan of gently simmering water. Spread the melted chocolate on the flat sides of the cookies and sandwich them together in pairs. Return to the wire racks to cool.

MAKES 20

175 g/6 oz butter

115 g/4 oz caster sugar

1 egg yolk

100 g/3½ oz ground almonds

175 g/6 oz plain flour

55 g/2 oz plain chocolate, broken into pieces

LEBKUCHEN

MAKES 60

3 eggs

200 g/7 oz golden caster sugar

55 g/2 oz plain flour

2 tsp cocoa powder

1 tsp ground cinnamon

1/2 tsp ground cardamom

1/4 tsp ground cloves

1/4 tsp ground nutmeg

175 g/6 oz ground almonds

55 g/2 oz chopped mixed peel,
   finely chopped

to decorate

115 g/4 oz plain chocolate

115 g/4 oz white chocolate

sugar crystals

Preheat the oven to 180°C/350°F/Gas Mark 4. Line several baking trays with baking paper.

Put the eggs and sugar in a heatproof bowl set over a saucepan of gently simmering water. Whisk until thick and foamy. Remove the bowl from the saucepan and continue to whisk for 2 minutes.

Sift the flour, cocoa powder, cinnamon, cardamom, cloves and nutmeg into the bowl and stir in with the ground almonds and mixed peel. Drop heaped teaspoonfuls of the mixture onto the prepared baking trays, spreading them gently into smooth mounds.

Bake in the preheated oven for 15–20 minutes, until light brown and slightly soft to the touch. Cool on the baking trays for 10 minutes, then transfer to wire racks to cool completely.

Put the plain and white chocolate in two separate heatproof bowls set over two saucepans of gently simmering water until melted. Dip half the biscuits in the melted plain chocolate and half in the white chocolate. Sprinkle with sugar crystals and leave to set.

BREAD & SAVOURY

CRUSTY WHITE BREAD

Place the egg and egg yolk in a jug and beat lightly to mix. Add enough lukewarm water to make up to 300 ml/10 fl oz. Stir well.

Place the flour, salt, sugar and yeast in a large bowl. Add the butter and rub it in with your fingertips until the mixture resembles breadcrumbs. Make a well in the centre, add the egg mixture and work to a smooth dough.

Turn out onto a lightly floured surface and knead well for about 10 minutes, until smooth. Brush a bowl with oil. Shape the dough into a ball, place it in the bowl and cover with a damp tea towel. Leave to rise in a warm place for 1 hour, until the dough has doubled in volume.

Preheat the oven to 220°C/425°F/Gas Mark 7. Oil a 900-g/ 2-lb loaf tin. Turn out the dough onto a lightly floured surface and knead for 1 minute until smooth. Shape the dough the length of the tin and three times the width. Fold the dough into three lengthways and place it in the tin with the join underneath. Cover and leave in a warm place for 30 minutes, until it has risen above the tin.

Place in the preheated oven and bake for 30 minutes, or until firm and golden brown. Test that the loaf is cooked by tapping on the base with your knuckles – it should sound hollow. Transfer to a wire rack to cool.

MAKES 1 LOAF

1 egg

1 egg yolk

150–200 ml/5–7 fl oz lukewarm water

500 g/1 lb 2 oz strong white flour, plus extra for dusting

1½ tsp salt

2 tsp sugar

1 tsp easy-blend dried yeast

25 g/1 oz butter, diced

sunflower oil, for greasing

WHOLEMEAL HARVEST BREAD

Place the flour, milk powder, salt, sugar and yeast in a large bowl. Pour in the oil and add the water, then mix well to make a smooth dough.

Turn out onto a lightly floured surface and knead well for about 10 minutes, until smooth. Brush a bowl with oil. Shape the dough into a ball, place it in the bowl and cover with a damp tea towel. Leave to rise in a warm place for 1 hour, until the dough has doubled in volume.

Preheat the oven to 220°C/425°F/Gas Mark 7. Oil a 900-g/ 2-lb loaf tin. Turn the dough out onto a lightly floured surface and knead for 1 minute, until smooth. Shape the dough the length of the tin and three times the width. Fold the dough into three lengthways and place it in the tin with the join underneath. Cover and leave in a warm place for 30 minutes, until it has risen above the tin.

Place in the preheated oven and bake for 30 minutes, or until firm and golden brown. Test that the loaf is cooked by tapping on the base with your knuckles – it should sound hollow. Transfer to a wire rack to cool.

MAKES 1 LOAF

225 g/8 oz strong wholemeal flour, plus extra for dusting

1 tbsp skimmed milk powder

1 tsp salt

2 tbsp soft light brown sugar

1 tsp easy-blend dried yeast

1½ tbsp sunflower oil, plus extra for greasing

175 ml/6 fl oz lukewarm water

MIXED SEED BREAD

MAKES 1 LOAF

375 g/13 oz strong white flour,
  plus extra for dusting

125 g/4½ oz rye flour

½ tbsp skimmed milk powder

½ tsp salt

tbsp soft light brown sugar

tsp easy-blend dried yeast

½ tbsp sunflower oil, plus extra
  for greasing

2 tsp lemon juice

300 ml/10 fl oz lukewarm water

tsp caraway seeds

½ tsp poppy seeds

½ tsp sesame seeds

topping

egg white

tbsp water

tbsp sunflower seeds
  or pumpkin seeds

Place the flours, milk powder, salt, sugar and yeast in a large
bowl. Pour in the oil and add the lemon juice and water. Stir in
the seeds and mix well to make a smooth dough. Turn out onto
a lightly floured surface and knead well for about 10 minutes,
until smooth.

Brush a bowl with oil. Shape the dough into a ball, place it
in the bowl and cover with a damp tea towel. Leave to rise in a
warm place for 1 hour, until the dough has doubled in volume.

Oil a 900-g/2-lb loaf tin. Turn out the dough onto a lightly
floured surface and knead for 1 minute until smooth. Shape the
dough the length of the tin and three times the width. Fold the
dough in three lengthways and place it in the tin with the join
underneath. Cover and leave in a warm place for 30 minutes,
until it has risen above the tin.

Preheat the oven to 220°C/425°F/Gas Mark 7. For the topping,
lightly beat the egg white with the water to make a glaze. Just
before baking, brush the glaze over the loaf, then gently press
the sunflower seeds all over the top.

Bake in the preheated oven for 30 minutes, or until firm and
golden brown. Test that the loaf is cooked by tapping on the base
with your knuckles – it should sound hollow. Transfer to a wire
rack to cool.

PLAITED POPPY SEED BREAD

Sift the flour and salt together into a bowl and stir in the milk powder, sugar and yeast. Make a well in the centre and pour in the lukewarm water and oil. Stir well with a wooden spoon until the dough begins to come together. Add the poppy seeds and knead with your hands until they are fully incorporated and the dough leaves the side of the bowl. Turn out onto a lightly floured surface and knead well for about 10 minutes, until smooth and elastic.

Brush a bowl with oil. Shape the dough into a ball, put it in the bowl and cover with a damp tea towel. Leave to rise in a warm place for 1 hour, until the dough has doubled in volume.

Brush a baking tray with oil. Turn out the dough onto a lightly floured surface, knock back with your fist and knead for 1–2 minutes. Divide the dough into three equal pieces and shape each into a rope 25–30 cm/10–12 inches long.

Place the ropes side by side and press them together at one end. Plait the dough, pinch the other end together and tuck it underneath. Put the loaf on the prepared baking tray. Cover the baking tray with a damp tea towel and leave to rise in a warm place for 30 minutes.

Preheat the oven to 200°C/400°F/Gas Mark 6. To make the topping, beat the egg yolk with the milk and sugar. Brush the egg glaze over the top of the loaf and sprinkle with the poppy seeds. Bake in the preheated oven for 30–35 minutes, until golden brown and the loaf sounds hollow when tapped on the base with your knuckles. Transfer to a wire rack to cool.

MAKES 1 LOAF

225 g/8 oz strong white flour, plus extra for dusting

1 tsp salt

2 tbsp skimmed milk powder

1½ tbsp caster sugar

1 tsp easy-blend dried yeast

175 ml/6 fl oz lukewarm water

2 tbsp vegetable oil, plus extra for brushing

5 tbsp poppy seeds

topping

1 egg yolk

1 tbsp milk

1 tbsp caster sugar

2 tbsp poppy seeds

RYE BREAD

Sift the flours and salt together into a bowl. Add the sugar and yeast and stir to mix. Make a well in the centre and pour in the lukewarm water and oil. Stir with a wooden spoon until the dough begins to come together, then knead with your hands until it leaves the side of the bowl. Turn out onto a lightly floured surface and knead for 10 minutes, until elastic and smooth.

Brush a bowl with oil. Shape the dough into a ball, put it in the bowl and cover with a damp tea towel. Leave to rise in a warm place for 2 hours, until the dough has doubled in volume.

Brush a baking tray with oil. Turn out the dough onto a lightly floured surface and knock back with your fist, then knead for a further 10 minutes. Shape the dough into a ball, put it on the prepared baking tray and cover with a damp tea towel. Leave to rise in a warm place for a further 40 minutes, until the dough has doubled in volume.

Meanwhile, preheat the oven to 190°C/375°F/Gas Mark 5. Beat the egg white with 1 tablespoon of water in a bowl. Bake the loaf in the preheated oven for 20 minutes, then remove from the oven and brush the top with the egg white glaze. Return to the oven and bake for a further 20 minutes. Brush the top of the loaf with the glaze again and return to the oven for a further 20–30 minutes, until the crust is a rich brown colour and the loaf sounds hollow when tapped on the base with your knuckles. Transfer to a wire rack to cool.

MAKES 1 LARGE LOAF

450 g/1 lb rye flour

225 g/8 oz strong white flour, plus extra for dusting

2 tsp salt

2 tsp soft light brown sugar

1½ tsp easy-blend dried yeast

425 ml/15 fl oz lukewarm water

2 tsp vegetable oil, plus extra for brushing

1 egg white

WALNUT & SEED BREAD

MAKES 2 LARGE LOAVES

450 g/1 lb wholemeal flour

450 g/1 lb granary flour

115 g/4 oz strong white flour, plus extra for dusting

2 tbsp sesame seeds

2 tbsp sunflower seeds

2 tbsp poppy seeds

115 g/4 oz walnuts, chopped

2 tsp salt

15 g/½ oz easy-blend dried yeast

2 tbsp olive oil or walnut oil

700 ml/1¼ pints lukewarm water

1 tbsp melted butter or oil, for greasing

In a mixing bowl, mix together the flours, seeds, walnuts, salt and yeast. Add the oil and lukewarm water and stir well to form a soft dough. Turn out the dough onto a lightly floured surface and knead well for 5–7 minutes. The dough should have a smooth appearance and feel elastic.

Return the dough to the bowl, cover with a damp tea towel and leave in a warm place for 1–1½ hours to rise.

When the dough has doubled in size, turn it out onto a lightly floured surface and knead again for 1 minute.

Grease two 900-g/2-lb loaf tins well with melted butter or oil. Divide the dough in two. Shape one piece the length of the tin and three times the width. Fold the dough in three lengthways and place in one of the tins with the join underneath. Repeat with the other piece of dough.

Cover and leave to rise again in a warm place for about 30 minutes, until the bread is well risen above the tins. Meanwhile, preheat the oven to 230°C/450°F/Gas Mark 8.

Bake in the centre of the preheated oven for 25–30 minutes. If the loaves are getting too brown, reduce the temperature to 220°C/425°F/Gas Mark 7. Test that the bread is cooked by tapping on the base with your knuckles – it should sound hollow. Transfer to a wire rack to cool.

IRISH SODA BREAD

Preheat the oven to 220ºC/425ºF/Gas Mark 7. Lightly grease a baking tray.

Sift the flour, salt and bicarbonate of soda into a mixing bowl. Make a well in the centre of the dry ingredients and pour in most of the buttermilk.

Mix well together using your hands. The dough should be very soft but not too wet. If necessary, add the remaining buttermilk.

Turn out the dough onto a lightly floured surface and knead it lightly. Shape into a 20-cm/8-inch round.

Place the bread on the prepared baking tray, cut a cross in the top and bake in the preheated oven for 25–30 minutes. Test that the loaf is cooked by tapping on the base with your knuckles – it should sound hollow.

MAKES 1 LOAF

butter, for greasing

450 g/1 lb plain flour, plus extra for dusting

1 tsp salt

1 tsp bicarbonate of soda

400 ml/14 fl oz buttermilk

CORN BREAD

Preheat the oven to 200°C/400°F/Gas Mark 6. Brush a 20-cm/ 8-inch square cake tin with oil.

Sift the flour, salt and baking powder together into a bowl. Add the sugar and polenta and stir to mix. Add the butter and cut it into the dry ingredients with a knife, then rub in with your fingertips until the mixture resembles breadcrumbs.

Lightly beat the eggs in a bowl with the milk and cream, then stir into the polenta mixture until thoroughly combined.

Spoon the mixture into the prepared tin and smooth the surface. Bake in the preheated oven for 30–35 minutes, until a skewer inserted into the centre of the loaf comes out clean. Remove the tin from the oven and leave to cool for 5–10 minutes, then cut into squares and serve warm.

MAKES 1 LOAF

vegetable oil, for brushing

175 g/6 oz plain flour

1 tsp salt

4 tsp baking powder

1 tsp caster sugar

280 g/10 oz polenta

115 g/4 oz butter, softened

4 eggs

250 ml/8 fl oz milk

3 tbsp double cream

CORIANDER & GARLIC NAAN

MAKES 3

280 g/10 oz strong white flour,
   plus extra for dusting

1 tsp salt

1 tbsp ground coriander

1 garlic clove, very finely chopped

1 tsp easy-blend dried yeast

2 tsp clear honey

100 ml/3½ fl oz lukewarm water

4 tbsp natural yogurt

1 tbsp vegetable oil, plus extra
   for brushing

1 tsp black onion seeds

1 tbsp chopped fresh coriander

Sift the flour, salt and ground coriander together into a bowl and stir in the garlic and yeast. Make a well in the centre and pour in the honey, water, yogurt and oil. Stir well with a wooden spoon until the dough begins to come together, then knead with your hands until it leaves the side of the bowl. Turn out onto a lightly floured surface and knead well for about 10 minutes, until smooth and elastic.

Brush a bowl with oil. Shape the dough into a ball, put it in the bowl and cover with a damp tea towel. Leave to rise in a warm place for 1–2 hours, until the dough has doubled in volume.

Put three baking trays in the oven and preheat to 240°C/475°F/Gas Mark 9. Preheat the grill. Turn out the dough onto a lightly floured surface and knock back with your fist. Divide the dough into three pieces, shape each piece into a ball and cover two of them with oiled clingfilm.

Roll out the uncovered piece of dough into a teardrop shape about 8 mm/⅜ inch thick and cover with oiled clingfilm. Roll out the other pieces of dough in the same way. Place the naan on the preheated baking trays and sprinkle with the onion seeds and chopped coriander. Bake in the preheated oven for 5 minutes, until puffed up. Transfer the naan bread to the grill pan, brush with oil and grill for 2–3 minutes. Serve warm.

TURKISH FLATBREAD

Sift the flour, salt, cumin and coriander together into a bowl and stir in the sugar and yeast. Make a well in the centre and pour in the oil and lukewarm water. Stir well with a wooden spoon until the dough begins to come together, then knead with your hands until it leaves the side of the bowl. Turn out onto a lightly floured surface and knead well for about 10 minutes, until smooth and elastic.

Brush a bowl with oil. Shape the dough into a ball, put it in the bowl and cover with a damp tea towel. Leave to rise in a warm place for 1 hour, until the dough has doubled in volume.

Lightly brush a baking tray with oil. Turn out the dough onto a lightly floured surface, knock back with your fist and knead for 1–2 minutes. Divide the dough into eight equal pieces, shape each piece into a ball, then roll out to a 20-cm/8-in round. Cover the rounds with a damp tea towel and leave to rest for 20 minutes.

Heat a heavy-based frying pan and brush the base with oil. Add one dough round, cover and cook for 2–3 minutes, until lightly browned on the underside. Turn over with a fish slice, re-cover the pan and cook for a further 2 minutes, until lightly browned on the second side. Remove from the pan and cook the remaining dough rounds in the same way.

MAKES 8

750 g/1 lb 10 oz plain flour, plus extra for dusting

1½ tsp salt

1 tsp ground cumin

½ tsp ground coriander

1 tsp caster sugar

7 g/¼ oz easy-blend dried yeast

2 tbsp olive oil, plus extra for brushing

400 ml/14 fl oz lukewarm water

TOMATO & ROSEMARY FOCACCIA

Sift the flour and salt together into a bowl and stir in the yeast and rosemary. Make a well in the centre, pour in 4 tablespoons of the oil and mix quickly with a wooden spoon. Gradually stir in the lukewarm water but do not overmix. Turn out onto a lightly floured surface and knead for 2 minutes. The dough will be quite wet; do not add more flour.

Brush a bowl with oil. Shape the dough into a ball, put it in the bowl and cover with a damp tea towel. Leave to rise in a warm place for 2 hours, until the dough has doubled in volume.

Brush a baking tray with oil. Turn out the dough onto a lightly floured surface and knock back with your fist, then knead for 1 minute. Put the dough on the prepared baking tray and press out into an even layer. Cover the baking tray with a damp tea towel. Leave to rise in a warm place for 1 hour.

Preheat the oven to 240°C/475°F/Gas Mark 9. Cut the tomato halves in half. Whisk the remaining oil with a little water in a bowl. Dip your fingers into the oil mixture and press them into the dough to make dimples all over the loaf. Sprinkle with the sea salt. Press the tomato quarters into some of the dimples, drizzle with the remaining oil mixture and sprinkle the loaf with the rosemary sprigs.

Reduce the oven temperature to 220°C/425°F/Gas Mark 7 and bake in the preheated oven for 20 minutes, until golden brown. Transfer to a wire rack to cool slightly, then serve while still warm.

MAKES 1 LOAF

500 g/1 lb 2 oz strong white flour, plus extra for dusting

1½ tsp salt

1½ tsp easy-blend dried yeast

2 tbsp chopped fresh rosemary, plus extra sprigs to garnish

6 tbsp extra virgin olive oil, plus extra for brushing

300 ml/10 fl oz lukewarm water

6 oven-dried or sun-blush tomato halves

1 tsp coarse sea salt

BASIC PIZZA DOUGH

SERVES 2–4

175 g/6 oz plain flour, plus extra
   for dusting

1 tsp salt

1 tsp easy-blend dried yeast

1 tbsp olive oil, plus extra
   for brushing and drizzling

6 tbsp lukewarm water

topping

175 ml/6 fl oz ready-made pizza
   tomato sauce or 350 g/12 oz
   tomatoes, peeled and halved

1 garlic clove, thinly sliced

55 g/2 oz mozzarella cheese,
   thinly sliced

1 tsp dried oregano

salt and pepper

fresh basil sprigs, to garnish

Sift the flour and salt together into a bowl and stir in the yeast. Make a well in the centre and pour in the oil and lukewarm water. Stir well with a wooden spoon until the dough begins to come together, then knead with your hands until it leaves the side of the bowl. Turn out onto a lightly floured surface and knead well for 5–10 minutes, until smooth and elastic.

Brush a bowl with oil. Shape the dough into a ball, put it in the bowl and cover with a damp tea towel. Leave to rise in a warm place for 1 hour, until the dough has doubled in volume.

Brush a baking tray with oil. Turn out the dough onto a lightly floured surface, knock back with your fist and knead for 1 minute. Roll or press out the dough to a 25-cm/10-inch round. Place on the prepared baking tray and push up the edge slightly all round. Cover the baking tray with a damp tea towel and leave to rise in a warm place for 10 minutes.

Preheat the oven to 200°C/400°F/Gas Mark 6. Spread the tomato sauce, if using, over the pizza base almost to the edge. If using fresh tomatoes, squeeze out some of the juice and roughly chop the flesh. Spread them evenly over the pizza base and drizzle with oil. Sprinkle the garlic over the tomato, add the cheese, sprinkle with the oregano and season with salt and pepper. Bake in the preheated oven for 15–20 minutes, until the crust is golden brown and crisp. Brush the crust with oil, garnish with basil sprigs and serve immediately.

ENGLISH MUFFINS

Sift the flour and salt together into a bowl and stir in the sugar and yeast. Make a well in the centre and add the water and yogurt. Stir with a wooden spoon until the dough begins to come together, then knead with your hands until it comes away from the side of the bowl. Turn out onto a lightly floured surface and knead for 5–10 minutes, until smooth and elastic.

Brush a bowl with oil. Shape the dough into a ball, put it in the bowl and cover with a damp tea towel. Leave to rise in a warm place for 30–40 minutes, until the dough has doubled in volume.

Dust a baking tray with flour. Turn out the dough onto a lightly floured surface and knead lightly. Roll out to a thickness of 2 cm/ ¾ inch. Stamp out 10–12 rounds with a 7.5-cm/3-inch biscuit cutter and sprinkle each round with semolina. Transfer the muffins to the prepared baking tray, cover with a damp tea towel and leave to rise in a warm place for 30–40 minutes.

Heat a griddle or large frying pan over a medium–high heat and brush lightly with oil. Add half the muffins and cook for 7–8 minutes on each side, until golden brown. Cook the remaining muffins in the same way.

MAKES 10–12

450 g/1 lb strong white bread flour, plus extra for dusting

½ tsp salt

1 tsp caster sugar

1½ tsp easy-blend dried yeast

250 ml/9 fl oz lukewarm water

125 ml/4 fl oz natural yogurt

vegetable oil, for brushing

40 g/1½ oz semolina

BAGELS

Sift the flour and salt together into a bowl and stir in the yeast. Make a well in the centre, pour in the egg and the lukewarm water and mix to a dough. Turn out onto a lightly floured surface and knead well for about 10 minutes, until smooth.

Brush a bowl with oil. Shape the dough into a ball, place it in the bowl and cover with a damp tea towel. Leave to rise in a warm place for 1 hour, until the dough has doubled in volume.

Brush two baking trays with oil and dust a tray with flour. Turn out the dough onto a lightly floured surface and knock back with your fist. Knead for 2 minutes, then divide into ten pieces. Shape each piece into a ball and leave to rest for 5 minutes. Gently flatten each ball with a lightly floured hand and make a hole in the centre with the handle of a wooden spoon. Put the bagels on the floured tray, cover with a damp tea towel and leave to rise in a warm place for 20 minutes.

Meanwhile, preheat the oven to 220°C/425°F/Gas Mark 7 and bring a large saucepan of water to the boil. Reduce the heat until the water is barely simmering, then add two bagels. Poach for 1 minute, then turn over and poach for a further 30 seconds. Remove with a slotted spoon and drain on a tea towel. Poach the remaining bagels in the same way.

Transfer the bagels to the prepared baking trays. Beat the egg white with the water in a bowl and brush it over the bagels. Sprinkle with the caraway seeds and bake in the preheated oven for 25–30 minutes, until golden brown. Transfer to a wire rack to cool.

MAKES 10

350 g/12 oz strong white flour, plus extra for dusting

2 tsp salt

7 g/¼ oz easy-blend dried yeast

1 tbsp lightly beaten egg

200 ml/7 fl oz lukewarm water

vegetable oil, for brushing

1 egg white

2 tsp water

2 tbsp caraway seeds

BREADSTICKS

MAKES 30

350 g/12 oz strong white flour,
   plus extra for dusting

1½ tsp salt

1½ tsp easy-blend dried yeast

200 ml/7 fl oz lukewarm water

3 tbsp olive oil, plus extra
   for brushing

sesame seeds, for coating

Sift the flour and salt together into a warmed bowl. Stir in the yeast. Make a well in the centre. Add the water and oil to the well and mix to form a soft dough.

Turn out the dough onto a lightly floured work surface and knead for 5–10 minutes, or until smooth and elastic. Put the dough in an oiled bowl, cover with a damp tea towel and leave to rise in a warm place for 1 hour, or until doubled in size.

Preheat the oven to 200°C/400°F/Gas Mark 6. Lightly oil two baking trays.

Turn out the dough again and knead lightly. Roll out into a rectangle measuring 23 x 20 cm/9 x 8 inches. Cut the dough into three strips, each 20 cm/8 inches long, then cut each strip across into ten equal pieces.

Gently roll and stretch each piece of dough into a stick about 30 cm/12 inches long, then brush with oil. Spread out the sesame seeds on a large shallow plate or tray. Roll each breadstick in the sesame seeds to coat, then space well apart on the prepared baking trays. Brush with oil, cover with a damp tea towel and leave to prove in a warm place for 15 minutes.

Bake the breadsticks in the preheated oven for 10 minutes. Turn over and bake for a further 5–10 minutes, until golden. Transfer to a wire rack and leave to cool.

CHEESE
STRAWS

Sift the flour, salt and curry powder into a bowl. Add the butter
and rub in until the mixture resembles breadcrumbs. Add the
cheese and half the egg and mix to form a dough. Wrap in
clingfilm and chill in the refrigerator for 30 minutes.

Preheat the oven to 200°C/400°F/Gas Mark 6, then grease
several baking trays. On a floured work surface, roll out the
dough to 5 mm/¼ inch thick. Cut into 7.5 x 1-cm/3 x ½-inch
strips. Pinch the strips lightly along the sides and place on the
prepared baking trays.

Brush the strips with the remaining egg and sprinkle half
with poppy seeds and half with cumin seeds. Bake in the
preheated oven for 10–15 minutes, or until golden. Transfer
to wire racks to cool.

MAKES 24

115 g/4 oz plain flour, plus extra
    for dusting

pinch of salt

1 tsp curry powder

55 g/2 oz butter, plus extra
    for greasing

55 g/2 oz grated Cheddar cheese

1 egg, beaten

poppy and cumin seeds,
    for sprinkling

SAVOURY OAT
CRACKERS

Preheat the oven to 180°C/350°F/Gas Mark 4. Lightly grease two baking trays.

Rub the butter into the oats and flour, using your fingertips. Stir in the salt, thyme and walnuts, then add the egg and mix to a soft dough. Spread out the sesame seeds on a large shallow plate or tray. Break off walnut-sized pieces of dough and roll into balls, then roll in the sesame seeds to coat lightly and evenly.

Place the balls of dough on the prepared baking trays, spacing well apart, and roll the rolling pin over them to flatten as much as possible. Bake in the preheated oven for 12–15 minutes, or until firm and pale golden.

Cool on the baking trays for 3–4 minutes, then transfer to a wire rack to finish cooling.

MAKES 12–14

100 g/3½ oz unsalted butter, plus extra for greasing

90 g/3¼ oz rolled oats

25 g/1 oz wholemeal flour

½ tsp coarse sea salt

1 tsp dried thyme

40 g/1½ oz walnuts, finely chopped

1 egg, beaten

40 g/1½ oz sesame seeds

CHEESE SABLÉS

MAKES 35

150 g/5½ oz plain flour, plus extra for dusting

150 g/5½ oz mature Cheddar cheese, grated

150 g/5½ oz butter, diced, plus extra for greasing

1 egg yolk

sesame seeds, for sprinkling

Mix the flour and cheese together in a bowl. Add the butter to the cheese and flour mixture and rub in with your fingertips until combined.

Stir in the egg yolk and mix to form a dough. Wrap the dough in clingfilm and leave to chill in the refrigerator for about 30 minutes.

Preheat the oven to 200°C/400°F/Gas Mark 6. Lightly grease several baking trays.

On a lightly floured surface, roll out the dough thinly. Stamp out 6-cm/2½-inch rounds with a biscuit cutter, re-rolling the trimmings to make about 35 rounds.

Place the rounds on the prepared baking trays and sprinkle the sesame seeds over the top of them.

Bake in the preheated oven for 10 minutes, until the sablés are light golden in colour. Carefully transfer the cheese sablés to a wire rack and leave to cool slightly before serving.

CHEESE & MUSTARD SCONES

Preheat the oven to 220°C/425°F/Gas Mark 7. Lightly grease a baking tray.

Sift the flour, baking powder and salt into a mixing bowl. Rub in the butter with your fingertips until the mixture resembles breadcrumbs.

Stir in the cheese, mustard and enough milk to form a soft dough.

On a lightly floured surface, knead the dough very lightly, then flatten it out with the palm of your hand to a depth of about 2.5 cm/1 inch.

Cut the dough into eight wedges with a knife. Brush each one with a little milk and sprinkle with pepper to taste.

Bake in a the preheated oven for 10–15 minutes, until golden brown. Transfer the scones to a wire rack and leave to cool slightly before serving.

MAKES 8

50 g/1¾ butter, diced, plus extra for greasing

225 g/8 oz self-raising flour, plus extra for dusting

1 tsp baking powder

pinch of salt

125 g/4½ oz mature Cheddar cheese, grated

1 tsp mustard powder

150 ml/5 fl oz milk, plus extra for brushing

pepper

PARMESAN & PINE KERNEL MUFFINS

Preheat the oven to 200°C/400°F/Gas Mark 6. Grease a 12-cup muffin tin or line with 12 paper muffin cases.

To make the topping, mix together the Parmesan cheese and pine kernels and set aside.

To make the muffins, sift together the flour, baking powder, and salt and pepper to taste into a large bowl. Stir in the Parmesan cheese and pine kernels.

Lightly beat the eggs in a large jug or bowl then beat in the buttermilk and oil. Make a well in the centre of the dry ingredients and pour in the beaten liquid ingredients. Stir gently until just combined; do not over-mix.

Spoon the mixture into the prepared muffin tin. Scatter the topping over the muffins. Bake in the preheated oven for about 20 minutes, until well risen, golden brown and firm to the touch.

Leave the muffins in the tin for 5 minutes, then serve warm.

MAKES 12

oil or melted butter,
   for greasing (if using)

280 g/10 oz plain flour

1 tbsp baking powder

⅛ tsp salt

85 g/3 oz freshly grated Parmesan
   cheese

60 g/2¼ oz pine kernels

2 eggs

250 ml/9 fl oz buttermilk

6 tbsp sunflower oil or 85 g/
   3 oz butter, melted and cooled

pepper

topping
10 g/¼ oz freshly grated
   Parmesan cheese

35 g/1¼ oz pine kernels

CARAMELIZED ONION MUFFINS

MAKES 12

oil or melted butter,
    for greasing (if using)

7 tbsp sunflower oil

3 onions, finely chopped

1 tbsp red wine vinegar

2 tsp sugar

280 g/10 oz plain flour

1 tbsp baking powder

⅛ tsp salt

2 eggs

250 ml/9 fl oz buttermilk

pepper

Preheat the oven to 200°C/400°F/Gas Mark 6. Grease a 12-cup muffin tin or line with 12 paper muffin cases.

Heat 2 tablespoons of the oil in a frying pan. Add the onions and cook for about 3 minutes, until beginning to soften. Add the vinegar and sugar and cook, stirring occasionally, for a further 10 minutes, until golden brown. Remove from the heat and leave to cool.

Meanwhile, sift together the flour, baking powder, and salt and pepper to taste into a large bowl.

Lightly beat the eggs in a large jug or bowl then beat in the buttermilk and the remaining oil. Make a well in the centre of the dry ingredients, pour in the beaten liquid ingredients and add the onion mixture, reserving 4 tablespoons for the topping. Stir gently until just combined; do not over-mix.

Spoon the mixture into the prepared muffin tin. Sprinkle the reserved onion mixture on top of the muffins. Bake in the preheated oven for about 20 minutes, until well risen, golden brown and firm to the touch.

Leave the muffins in the tin for 5 minutes, then serve warm.

TRIPLE TOMATO TART

To make the puff pastry, sift the flour and salt into a large mixing bowl and rub in 25 g/1 oz of the butter. Gradually add the water, just enough to bring the pastry together, and knead briefly to a smooth dough. Wrap in clingfilm and chill for 30 minutes.

Wrap the remaining butter in clingfilm and shape it into a 3 cm/1¼ inch thick rectangle. Roll out the dough to a rectangle three times longer and 3 cm/1¼ inches wider than the butter and place the butter in the centre with the long side towards you. Fold over the two 'wings' of pastry to enclose the butter – press down the edges to seal and then turn the pastry so the short side faces you. Roll the pastry to its original length, fold in three, turn and roll again to its original length. Repeat this once more and then rewrap the pastry and chill again for 30 minutes. Remove from the refrigerator and repeat the rolling and turning twice more. Chill again for 30 minutes.

Preheat the oven to 190°C/375°F/Gas Mark 5. Roll out the pastry to 35 x 25 cm/14 x 10 inches and place on a baking tray. Spread the sun-dried tomato purée over the pastry, leaving a 3-cm/1¼-inch margin around the edge. Arrange the tomato slices over the tart, scatter over the tomato halves, top with the rosemary and drizzle with 1 tablespoon of the oil and the vinegar. Brush the edges of the pastry with the egg yolk, place in the preheated oven and bake for 10 minutes. Scatter over the salami and bake for a further 10–15 minutes. Season to taste with salt and pepper, drizzle with the remaining oil and garnish with thyme.

SERVES 6

pastry

175 g/6 oz plain flour

pinch of salt

175 g/6 oz unsalted butter

about 150 ml/5 fl oz chilled water

(or use 250 g/9 oz ready-made puff pastry)

topping

3 tbsp sun-dried tomato purée

250 g/9 oz ripe vine tomatoes, sliced

150 g/5½ oz cherry tomatoes, cut in half

2 fresh rosemary sprigs, chopped

2 tbsp extra virgin olive oil

1 tbsp balsamic vinegar

1 egg yolk

125 g/4½ oz Italian sliced salami, chopped

salt and pepper

fresh thyme sprigs, to garnish

FETA & SPINACH TARTLETS

Grease six 9-cm/3½-inch loose-based round tart tins. Sift the flour and salt into a food processor, add the butter and process until the mixture resembles fine breadcrumbs. Tip the mixture into a large bowl and add the nutmeg and enough cold water to bring the dough together.

Preheat the oven to 200°C/400°F/Gas Mark 6. Turn out the dough onto a floured surface and divide into six equal-sized pieces. Roll each piece to fit the tart tins. Carefully fit each piece of pastry in its case and press well to fit the tin. Roll the rolling pin over the tin to neaten the edges and trim the excess pastry. Cut out six pieces of baking paper and fit a piece into each tart, fill with baking beans and chill in the refrigerator for 30 minutes.

Bake the tart cases blind in the preheated oven for 10 minutes, then remove the beans and paper.

Blanch the spinach in boiling water for just 1 minute, then drain and press to squeeze all the water out. Chop the spinach. Melt the butter in a frying pan, add the spinach and cook gently to evaporate any remaining liquid. Season well with salt and pepper. Stir in the cream and egg yolks. Crumble the cheese and divide between the tarts, top with the spinach mixture and bake for 10 minutes. Scatter the pine kernels over the tartlets and cook for a further 5 minutes.

MAKES 6

pastry
125 g/4½ oz plain flour, plus extra for dusting

pinch of salt

75 g/2½ oz cold butter, cut into pieces, plus extra for greasing

½ tsp ground nutmeg

1–2 tbsp cold water

filling
250 g/9 oz baby spinach

25 g/1 oz butter

150 ml/5 fl oz double cream

3 egg yolks

125 g/4½ oz feta cheese

50 g/1¾ oz pine kernels

salt and pepper

QUICHE LORRAINE

SERVES 4

pastry

200 g/7 oz plain flour, plus extra
   for dusting

100 g/3½ oz salted butter

1–2 tbsp cold water

filling

15 g/½ oz butter

1 small onion, finely chopped

4 lean streaky bacon rashers,
   diced

55 g/2 oz Gruyère cheese or
   Cheddar cheese, grated

2 eggs, beaten

300 ml/10 fl oz single cream

pepper

For the pastry, sift the flour into a bowl and rub in the butter with your fingertips until the mixture resembles fine breadcrumbs. Stir in just enough water to bind the mixture to a firm dough.

Roll out the dough on a lightly floured surface to a round slightly larger than a 23-cm/9-inch loose-based round tart tin, 3 cm/1¼ inches deep. Lift the pastry onto the tin and press it down into the fluted edge, using the back of your finger. Roll the rolling pin over the edge of the tin to trim off the excess pastry. Prick the base all over with a fork. Chill in the refrigerator for at least 10 minutes to allow the pastry to rest and prevent shrinkage.

Preheat the oven to 200°C/400°C/Gas Mark 6 and preheat a baking tray. Place a sheet of baking paper in the pastry-lined tin. Fill with baking beans to weigh it down. Place on the baking tray and bake in the preheated oven for 10 minutes. Remove the paper and beans and bake for a further 10 minutes.

For the filling, melt the butter in a frying pan and cook the onion and bacon over a medium heat for about 5 minutes, stirring occasionally, until the onion is softened and lightly browned. Spread the mixture evenly in the hot pastry case and sprinkle with half the cheese. Beat together the eggs and cream in a small bowl and season to taste with pepper. Pour into the pastry case and sprinkle with the remaining cheese.

Reduce the oven temperature to 190°C/375°F/Gas Mark 5. Place the quiche in the oven and bake for 25–30 minutes, or until golden brown and just set. Cool for 10 minutes before turning out.

INDEX